"When politics has the attenti[...] ut of the supernatural, it leaves us with the dry desert of the *natural*. In heaven the supernatural is the natural, for everything is *super* in the absence of the natural. Through modern day Elijahs, we may once again experience the *super* in our natural and amaze this world back to God. The absence of the supernatural is the main reason why showmanship has replaced supernatural anointing for the church. God will once again restore the rain through modern-day prophets who will alert the church one more time to the *super* that we so desperately need in our natural. Mark Ivey's voice through this book can be heard as a cry on behalf of the church to draw us back to the true, authentic prophetic Elijah voices of this modern day. I salute you, Mark, for releasing this cry through this book in a day when most prefer to play it safe. The world and even the church is content with business as usual and only the Elijah cry will bring back Jesus' glory in this modern day. May God transform everyone who reads this book into another Elijah to take responsibility and speak forth God's oracles of truth. Fire and rain is in the forecast for this dry and weary day."

Andre van Zyl, author, prophetic voice
Founder, Good News to the Nations, Inc., The Upper Room, www.gnni.org

"There are some books that present great teaching and some that are a great read. Seldom do you find a book that accomplishes both, but *The Elijahs of God* does just that! My friend, Pastor Mark Ivey, has written a book that is timely and relevant for the day and culture that we find ourselves in in America, both politically and in the church. The very first chapter is going to hook you into prophetic truth that every American Christian needs to hear! Pastor Ivey's book brings to my mind a phrase we have all heard at one time or another: Let the church be the church! Congratulations, Pastor Mark Ivey, for reminding all of us that Jesus is still and always will be the answer, not politics!"
Bishop David L. Thomas
Victory Christian Center, NXL Network

"We are living in a crucial hour when deception is sweeping into the church at unprecedented levels. The need for the Elijahs of God to rise and confront the trending patterns of Baal worship and spiritual compromise has never been greater. I thank God for a spiritual leader like Mark Ivey who has articulated with profound clarity many of the current issues in the church, but also provides healthy solutions and hope for a tremendous outpouring of the Holy

Spirit that is to come. As an international traveling prophetic minister and having the privilege to know Mark on a personal level, I can assure you that what you are about to read is simply an overflow of what God has put deep down inside of this man. I encourage everyone to get this book and apply its truths to your life and with as many other people as you know."
Jeremiah Johnson
Founder of Behold the Man Ministries

"Pastor Mark Ivey has written a now word for the church in America that every pastor and Christian must read as we are facing a continuous moral decline in a biblically illiterate country. His parallel between the confrontation on Mount Carmel in 1 Kings 17-19 between Elijah and Baal worshipers masterfully contrasts the church in America, which is desperately battling to survive in a relativistic, compromising culture which chooses to ignore the warning signs of Almighty God's judgments. *The Elijahs of God* is a powerful cry for God's people to restore their personal altar time; live in holiness and righteousness; and overcome the spirit of Jezebel in the church and our land, which will usher in "worldwide spiritual authority" as prophesied in Revelation 2:26-28. Moreover, Pastor Mark emphasizes the urgency to "grasp that anointing and calling are generational" and that present-day Elijahs must leave a legacy to the young, upcoming Elishas who are in every church. I am highly honored to endorse and recommend *The Elijahs of God*."
David A. Garcia, author and pastor
Grace World Outreach Church, Brooksville, Florida

"This is a book that will make you think. This is a book that will challenge your preconceived notions of politics. This is a book that draws unmistakable parallels to the days we are living in and the days of Elijah. *The Elijahs of God* is written to provoke us to rebuild the altar, to confront the Jezebel spirit that pervades our nation and culture, and expect the divine intervention that comes only from God's giving hand! To every pastor or congregant, if you're looking for a reason to "press in" and transfer the mantle of faith to your sons and daughters, this book may be the spark that sets your world on fire! We need revival! Thank you, Mark, for taking the time to seek God and communicate the obvious. I pray we will listen."
Phillip Cameron
Founder, The Orphan's Hands

"I have known Pastor Mark Ivey for over thirty years. His passion to know God and His heartbeat for the church, I believe, is expressed in his new book, *The Elijahs of God*. It is straightforward and balanced, a 'now word' for the church. I recommend we not only read but ask the Holy Spirit what He might have to say to us on an individual basis through *The Elijahs of God*."
Pastor Steve Burks
Lead Pastor, First Assembly of God, New Albany Indiana

"Mark Ivey looks and finds the voice of God in America through the ancient story of Elijah. He has ventured into territory that few authors have traveled. This book will provoke you to get back to the basics."
Dr. Michael Rakes, author
Pastor, Winston Salem First, Winston-Salem, NC

THE ELIJAHS OF GOD

Why the American Church Must Move Beyond Politics into Supernatural Awakening

Mark Ivey

5 Fold Media
Visit us at www.5foldmedia.com

The Elijahs of God: Why the American Church Must Move Beyond Politics into Supernatural Awakening
Copyright 2017 by Mark Ivey
Published by 5 Fold Media, LLC
www.5foldmedia.com

Unless otherwise indicated, all Scripture quotations are taken from the Holy Bible, *New Living Translation,* copyright © 1996, 2004, 2007, 2013, 2015 by Tyndale House Foundation. Used by permission of Tyndale House Publishers, Inc., Carol Stream, Illinois 60188. All rights reserved.

Scripture quotations marked (NIV) are taken from the Holy Bible, *New International Version®*, NIV®. Copyright © 1973, 1978, 1984, 2011 by Biblica, Inc.™ Used by permission of Zondervan. All rights reserved worldwide. www.zondervan.com The "NIV" and "New International Version" are trademarks registered in the United States Patent and Trademark Office by Biblica, Inc.™

Scripture quotations marked NASB are taken from the *New American Standard Bible®* (NASB), Copyright © 1960, 1962, 1963, 1968, 1971, 1972, 1973, 1975, 1977, 1995 by The Lockman Foundation. Used by permission. www.Lockman.org.

Scripture quotations marked MSG are taken from *The Message*. Copyright © 1993, 1994, 1995, 1996, 2000, 2001, 2002. Used by permission of NavPress Publishing Group.

Scripture quotations marked "NKJV™" are taken from the *New King James Version®*. Copyright © 1982 by Thomas Nelson, Inc. Used by permission. All rights reserved.

Front cover design by Ashton Ivey.

ISBN: 978-1-942056-40-9

Library of Congress Control Number: 2017932194

Dedication

The writing of any book is more than a compilation of information but the treasury of one's life experiences and those who have had the greatest impact and influence over long periods of time. I am grateful beyond words to dedicate *The Elijahs of God* to my family for allowing me the time and effort to spend long hours in front of a screen to produce the book you now hold in your hand.

To my wife Tiffany: You are an amazing gift from God. Your sensitivity to the Lord, candor, and willingness to follow the Lord wherever He has led us has made ministry with you a delight; and your skills as a mother have forever shaped our children. You have helped guide every part of my life, and I love you dearly for who you are and what you mean to me.

To my daughter Ariel: You are truly a princess. Your creativity continually amazes me, and your gifts are beyond my ability to accurately list. I could not have asked for a more perfect young lady. May you and your husband Jordan be blessed with the fatness of heaven's riches as you develop your life together.

To my elder son Ashton: I am so proud of the man you have become. God's grace is upon your life and your many skills keep multiplying with everything you touch. Your energy is amazing and heart for worship inspiring. May all the Lord's dreams in your heart today become reality.

To my younger son Caymen: Your life has been marked by the hand of God himself. As the "voice out of nowhere," your humor and wisdom

7

The Elijahs of God

will become evident to everyone around you. You are an awesome and gracious young man with gifts yet to come forth and be a blessing to many people. I'm grateful to God for who you are.

To all of our children: You are our beloved sons and daughter in whom we are well pleased. All of you are "Elijahs of God" with a resounding voice that will shout the freedom of Jesus to the nations. I love you dearly.

Acknowledgements

Thanks to Christ Alive Church, who are the most amazing people to pastor in America.

To my staff, whose heart for national awakening is contagious—you are awesome to work with every day.

To the many friends who have influenced my life and have graciously endorsed this book; to my wonderful mom for her help with *The Elijahs of God* and for always believing in me. You are the sweetest lady I know.

To my extended family who although kept apart by distance are always close in heart.

To 5 Fold Media for understanding the significance of prophetic writing and being one of the great Christian publishers in America. Thank you for all your help.

And to my grandmother, Jean Sewell, affectionately known as Sister Sewell. Thank you for praying me into the kingdom and leaving a godly legacy. I will see you in heaven one day.

Contents

Foreword

In his new book, *The Elijahs of God*, my dear friend, pastor, and prophetic voice, Mark Ivey has fired a shot across the bow of the enemy. With a no retreat mentality and passion for revival, Mark declares to the bride of Christ that we must, "*Wake up, sleeper, rise from the dead, and Christ will shine on you*" (Ephesians 5:14 NIV). This book is destined to be a classic. It has been written for all those willing to die for more of Jesus and live as if we have no tomorrow. I believe that *The Elijahs of God* is a modern day revivalist's handbook for victory!

As I read through the pages my heart was deeply stirred. This book is not only a road map for personal revival but also a message to America that our time is running out! I believe that there is a mighty awakening of Holy Spirit revival coming to our land. With this awakening will surely come the greatest attack from Satan that has ever been seen. The attack will be different from what we have seen in the past. It will be a subtle release of toxic, perverted, mindless bile released through the airwaves, the lecture podium, and the culture police who are hell bent on stamping out anything to do with Christianity. This will lead to the rise of an antichrist agenda and the Belial (lawlessness) spirit of 2 Corinthians 6:14-15. We must have an Isaiah 58:1 declaration: "*Shout it aloud, do not hold back. Raise your voice like a trumpet. Declare to my people their rebellion and to the descendants of Jacob their sins*" (NIV). Will you "Cry aloud and spare not"? Mark teaches us that we must change the narrative being espoused from those who only preach from memories of yesterday's glory and not the humility and aroma of a recent encounter with a "new every morning" Savior!

The Elijahs of God

He reminds us that we must determine that our cries for revival matter more than the retribution of the religiously satisfied and the voices of lost holiness. Jesus said in Matthew 12:30, "*This is war, and there is no neutral ground. If you're not on my side, you're the enemy; if you're not helping, you're making things worse*" (MSG).

Mark reminds us that we must consecrate ourselves and make ready for battle. The confrontation between good and evil now stands on our doorsteps. It was a fiery confrontation between good and evil on Mount Carmel in 1 Kings 18 that brought forth an awesome response from God. His holy fire fell and made a show of the enemy. This confrontation between the prophet of God and the prophets of Baal was the beginning of the end for Jezebel and Ahab! It all started with a weary prophet who had an awakening that God was demanding more from him. The Bible says Elijah the prophet stood alone, facing the enemies of God. Elijah passionately declared, "'*How long will you waver between two opinions? If the Lord is God, follow him; but if Baal is God, follow him.' But the people said nothing*" (1 Kings 18:21). How long will we continue to hear the sound of crickets from those God has entrusted with the message of redemption and truth? Dare we say to our kids that our nation was destroyed because those who had a voice decided the price to speak was more costly than their freedom? We must have the fire and the rain of Elijah's time once again!

God is looking for the Elijahs to not only rebuild the altar and confront the Jezebel spirit, but they must also be willing to lay their mantle on the next generation! Who are the Elijahs? These will be those who have been kissed by God with a holy fire and possess boldness to stand for truth! They will not be Christian celebrities or those man has determined have the right personas. They will be the cave dwellers who know the voice of God. Could it be that you are the one whom God has been waiting on? Maybe it was you, the reader, to whom God is referring in Malachi 4:5-6: "*I am sending you the prophet Elijah before the great and dreadful day of the Lord arrives. His preaching will turn the hearts of fathers to their children, and the hearts of children to their fathers. Otherwise I will come and strike the land with a curse.*"

Lastly, I must say a simple "thank you" to Mark for reminding this messenger of the gospel of peace that now is the time for war! Bravo, my friend!

Pat Schatzline
Evangelist and author of *I Am Remnant, Why Is God So Mad At Me?*,
and *Unqualified: Where You Can Begin to be Great*
Remnant Ministries International, raisetheremnant.com
Romans 11:5

It's Our Time

We must rise up and no longer disparage,
It's our time church to honour our heritage,
We have a Saviour who gave it all on the cross
As we stand beside martyrs who counted nothing but loss
They took God's mysteries and opened them up for us,
It's now our time to model His unending love.

Our mission is one we can't confuse
nor muddy up with some trite excuse.
You say you're not well versed ready or able,
I think Moses even tried to use that fable.
The time is now more urgent
if we should hear: Well done, good and faithful servant.

It's our time to confess the ways we were mangled
The sins and selfishness that had us entangled
Those paths led to our graves,
yet we return to our sins as if we were slaves.
Can we survive in this putrid Dead Sea?
I quote Paul, "May it never be!"

So let's cast aside our individual leprosy
and begin to live a biblical legacy.
There's a glorious prize waiting to be won
And the way to win is to start to run.

17

The Elijahs of God

Let's lace them up and fight the good fight
as we come to the world both salt and light.

Our life on earth is merely a vapour,
and we must move from pen to paper,
to help the world from her slumber awake.

Jesus, we are His beautiful bride,
Whom shall we fear with God on our side?
We have each other, we're not alone.
It's iron to iron in the combat zone.
There's a promise of life full of adventure
as long as we give both talent and treasure.

The workers are few, the harvest is plenty
With so many lives running on empty
Scores of people trying to cope,
As they come to an end of their proverbial rope.
Their eyes are wandering, seeking direction,
So make sure we point them to His resurrection.

Rise up, it's our time.

- Igniter Media[1]

---

1. This text is from a script that was written and produced by IgniterMedia.com. The video is called "It's Our Time."

Part 1:

The Elijahs of God are Rising

Chapter 1
It's Our Time

The story begins in 1 Kings 17. The Bible says, "*Now Elijah.*" What's interesting is that we don't know where the man came from or anything about his life. The only personal information we have about Elijah is that his name means "My God is Yahweh." It's as though he just showed up at a moment in time out of nowhere because it was God's time for him to show up. At particular crucial, difficult, challenging moments in history, God has raised up churches, organizations, and people young and old to confront the issues in their culture. From Abraham and the patriarchs, judges, prophets, priests and kings, apostles, founders of nations, and the unknown voices in small communities across America and the world—God has and will always have a voice.

And if there was ever a day when we needed the voice of God to trumpet a clear sound through those willing to speak, it is today. We have entered a period in history the Bible describes as perilous times. Paul wrote to a young pastor named Timothy and said:

> *You should know this, Timothy, that in the last days there will be very difficult times. For people will love only themselves and their money. They will be boastful and proud, scoffing at God, disobedient to their parents, and ungrateful. They will consider nothing sacred. They will be unloving and unforgiving; they will slander others and have no self-control. They will be cruel and hate what is good. They will betray their friends, be reckless, be*

puffed up with pride, and love pleasure rather than God.
They will act religious, but they will reject the power that
could make them godly. Stay away from people like that!
(2 Timothy 3:1-5)

With even a cursory glance at America, things do not seem, should I say, calm. An increase of lawlessness, shootings, riots, drug abuse, human trafficking, terrorism, persecution, political upheavals, and economic instability characterizes our day. A church more interested with being in the counsel of political candidates arguing for our position than in the counsel of God seeking His will tells us that "business as usual" is not going to bring us the peace we desire. Regardless of who we think should hold political office and the results of an election, we make a grave mistake when we look only to politicians for a guarantee of religious freedom and ultimately misunderstand the relationship between God and government.

> We make a grave mistake when we look only to politicians for a guarantee of religious freedom and ultimately misunderstand the relationship between God and government.

God established the offices of prophet, priest, and king to spiritually and governmentally guide the nation of Israel. The separation of these positions was important to God as a priest could not be a king, nor a king a priest. This separation kept ultimate power from resting in one individual. To have the spiritual and governmental offices in one person could potentially result in the corruption of both offices as would eventually happen. Both King Saul and King Uzziah were eventually removed from their positions for trying to operate in both spheres.[2] By the time of Christ, the priesthood was so corrupt and aligned with the political interests of the nation that a joining of the two would crucify their own Messiah.

---

2. Rev. Thomas C. Simcox, *Israel My Glory Magazine*, Volume 72, 2016, page 32.

This becomes a prophetic picture of the American church and a foreshadowing of the coming Antichrist. I watched a pastor on national television say that we need a president who will guarantee our religious freedom. What a mistake! When believers begin depending on political candidates to guarantee religious freedom, they unwittingly have linked two offices that God never intended to be joined together. It clearly shows how corrupt and backslidden American religion has become. The spirit of the antichrist, a political and religious governing system, has deceived millions of so-called Christians into denying the true power and protection of Christ and settling for man-made structures that will eventually oppose the very groups they were elected to protect.

We have equated conservatism and Christianity as one and the same when they may be very opposite. Conservatism is a political view that holds certain beliefs about morality, the involvement of government in the lives of people, financial spending, or other mores of society. It embraces a particular relationship to government. Christianity is about a relationship to Jesus and adherence to the Scriptures, regardless of political views. A conservative or liberal may or may not be a Christian. *To equate relationship with Jesus to a political view dumbs down the power of the gospel in any sphere of our culture.*

The idea that elections hold the key to an awakening is an American concept but is not found in the New Testament or in history. The first century church lived and ministered in one of the most hostile atmospheres to Christianity ever, yet they reached the known world in one generation! Historically, awakening precedes governmental change. It's not the other way around.

The House of Herod

At the start of the New Testament, we are introduced to a cast of Roman leaders. The first was a man named Herod the Great. He was a murderous, immoral, barbaric individual. Herod was so paranoid about retaining his position as king that he had his wife, her two sons, and his mother-in-law slain. Augustus Caesar said that it was safer to be Herod's pig than one of

The Elijahs of God

his own family. The joke was that since Herod did not eat pork, the pig, at least, would be safe. It is this man who was in charge when Jesus was born (see Matthew 2). You would think that God would choose a better time for His Son, the future eternal king, to come into the world. And yet, nothing could stop the plan of God. Through dreams and divine timing, God warned Joseph about Herod and saved Jesus' life from Herod's soldiers when they were sent to kill Him. Shortly after this event, historians tell us Herod died from a painful disease, yet the plan of God continued.

> The first century church lived and ministered in one of the most hostile atmospheres to Christianity ever, yet they reached the known world in one generation!

Herod Archelaus, son of Herod the Great, then took the reins of leadership. He immediately killed three thousand people during an uprising, continuing in his father's murderous ways. At this time, God warned Joseph again about this new Herod and Jesus' family went to live in Nazareth, fulfilling prophecy (Matthew 2:21). Because of his killing spree, Augustus Caesar had Herod banished and he died in obscurity while Jesus continued to grow in favor with God and men.

After this, Herod Antipas came to power—Herod the Great's youngest son by his Samaritan wife, Malthace. It was Herod Antipas who had John the Baptist beheaded (Mark 6:27). John was not a politically correct preacher. He confronted Herod for his incestuous marriage to Herodias, who was also his brother's wife! Herod put John in prison. It was while John the Baptist was imprisoned that Herodias's daughter performed a pornographic dance for Herod and he promised her anything she wanted. At the request of her mother, she asked for the head of John. This Herod was also the one who ruled during the ministry of Jesus and wanted Him killed (Luke 13:31). It was Herod Antipas who mocked Christ when He was brought to him the night before Jesus' crucifixion. Jesus was crucified and raised from the dead. Herod was banished and died and went into the history books as a lackluster little king, while Jesus sat down at the right hand of the Father and the church exploded in power!

Herod Agrippa I came next. This Herod joined in a political, religious alliance with the Jews to persecute Christians and had the apostle James martyred (Acts 12). Because he saw this pleased the Jewish establishment, he put Peter in prison as well, intending to have him killed after the Passover. But the church began to pray and God miraculously freed Peter. Acts 12 is a prophetic illustration of where the church is headed in America. Based on what is happening around the world and church history, I'm not convinced Americans will be exempt from persecution. It will be dangerous for Christians to relax over the next four years and think our faith will not be challenged. This is why the church must call for prayer like never before and not be caught by surprise. When the gospel is tested, the testing either drives us to compromise or moves us toward the Lord in prayer. The believers in Peter's time did not give up, and God responded with supernatural power. Shortly thereafter, Herod Agrippa I was judged by God for his failure to give God glory, and he died in agony while the gospel continued to spread.

Herod Agrippa II now found himself in a position of political influence. It was in front of this Herod that the apostle Paul made his defense before being sent to Rome (Acts 26). It is noteworthy that each of these Herods had an opportunity to receive Christ yet rejected the person of Jesus and forgiveness of sin!

Roman emperors were also not kind to Christianity. Both Peter and Paul were martyred under Nero. Gaius or Caligula was a violent, mentally unstable man, who tried to have a statue of himself erected in the temple at Jerusalem. The Jews said they would rather die than have his statue in their place of worship. It is understandable why they felt this way. What they did not know was that spiritually speaking, the system of temple worship with its animal sacrifices had ceased with the sacrifice of Jesus. In a short forty years, the temple itself would be completely destroyed by the army of Titus in AD 70.

The Elijahs of God

This presented a theological and political challenge for early Jewish Christians. Would they die for old religious, political, and spiritual paradigms of allegiance to a temple or give themselves completely to Christ and His eternal kingdom that had no end? Is it possible that God used this situation to separate those who had truly committed to Christ from unbelieving Jews who could not break away and fully surrender to the kingdom of God, regardless of what happened to their beloved temple? Could God be using our present political divisions among believers to separate those who are willing to die for temporal arguments and hope in men from those who have fully surrendered to the hope of God's kingdom? None of the ancient rulers or those of today are able to stop the spread of Christianity. Government does not rest on the shoulders of men but on Jesus Himself!

> *For a child is born to us, a son is given to us. The government will rest on his shoulders. And he will be called: Wonderful Counselor, Mighty God, Everlasting Father, Prince of Peace. His government and its peace will never end. He will rule with fairness and justice from the throne of his ancestor David for all eternity. The passionate commitment of the Lord of Heaven's Armies will make this happen!* (Isaiah 9:6-7)

I recently spent an evening in Charlotte, North Carolina where people were protesting the shooting of an African American man by an African American police officer. The crowds marched in circles for hours, chanting various political mantras to make their voices heard. After walking for about three hours and observing what was happening, it became evident the crowds were not only walking in circles physically but spiritually as well. The march would offer no solution. Our problems are not political but spiritual.

I'm not suggesting there aren't legitimate issues in need of answers. Cities must have a fair balance of justice and government does have a responsibility to protect its citizens, but there is clearly a tremendous amount of hurt being exhibited by a fatherless generation that is manifesting itself in anger. This is a spiritual problem. What we don't realize is that many of the moral battles of the day are fought on the political battlefield while the real fight is not natural but spiritual. Paul told the Ephesian church:

> *A final word: Be strong in the Lord and in his mighty power. Put on all of God's armor so that you will be able to stand firm against all strategies of the devil. For we are not fighting against flesh-and-blood enemies, but against evil rulers and authorities of the unseen world, against mighty powers in this dark world, and against evil spirits in the heavenly places* (Ephesians 6:10-12).

He told the church at Corinth, challenged by its own culture;

> *We are human, but we don't wage war as humans do. We use God's mighty weapons, not worldly weapons, to knock down the strongholds of human reasoning and to destroy false arguments. We destroy every proud obstacle that keeps people from knowing God. We capture their rebellious thoughts and teach them to obey Christ. And after you have become fully obedient, we will punish everyone who remains disobedient* (2 Corinthians 10:3-6).

> **What we don't realize is that many of the moral battles of the day are fought on the political battlefield while the real fight is not natural but spiritual.**

We always honor those God has placed in government because God's Word urges us to appreciate their service and realize the importance of their call to public service. But political weapons can only go so far. That's why Paul admonishes us to understand where the real battle is waged and begin to engage with the supernatural weapons Jesus has given us.

The Elijahs of God

We shouldn't blame politicians for the challenges in America. They are only a reflection of weak pulpits, preachers, and so-called Christians who have failed to declare the whole counsel of God. When the church agreed that there was more than one way to find God other than Jesus, declared morality was relative and not absolute, allowed that marriage was not just between a man and woman, conceded that animals' lives were more valuable than unborn babies, condemned the sins of society without dealing with our own, and pushed God out and let violence in, we opened the door to cultural confusion and chaos. Yet God continues to hold leaders in elected positions accountable for their actions and influence. God spoke through the prophet Micah and declared:

> *I said, "Listen, you leaders of Israel! You are supposed to know right from wrong, but you are the very ones who hate good and love evil. You skin my people alive and tear the flesh from their bones. Yes, you eat my people's flesh, strip off their skin, and break their bones. You chop them up like meat for the cooking pot. Then you beg the Lord for help in times of trouble! Do you really expect him to answer? After all the evil you have done, he won't even look at you!"* (Micah 3:1-4)

Those in elected offices cannot ignore God's will without consequence and neither can the body of Christ. National awakenings don't occur because of those in office though. Awakenings happen in response to the prayers of godly men and woman who have been crying to the Lord in private. American healing will not begin at the White House. We must come back to an altar of repentance in God's house for a fresh reality and hope of what a real relationship with Jesus can be. A great move of God is coming but will follow on the heels of national tragedy as people recognize the sovereign hand of God and respond to the prophetic voices of repentance in our land.

Churches and ministries who refuse to declare the whole counsel of God and are soft on sin and neglect righteous living will be sidelined by God, and the presence of Jesus that has been striving with them for years

28

will depart. Income will dry up and large buildings will become empty as those hungry for the real Jesus will seek out true voices that have been in the counsel of the Lord. Intimacy with Jesus will become priority over the business of ministry, and there will be a clear distinction between the godly and ungodly. This will create a new tension in American religion because chameleon Christians will no longer be able to blend in and hide spiritual duplicity anymore. Their lack of power will reveal their hypocrisy.

> We must get ready for what will happen on a national scale as the hand of God moves across the nation in simultaneous judgment and revival.

The Spirit of God will empower real believers with supernatural strength and street miracles, conversions and conviction of sin will draw people to the person of Jesus. There will be sovereign moves of God among Muslims in America and specific demographic groups. American millennials will experience Jesus by the tens of thousands, and just as the Jesus movement brought wayward children back to Christ, so the Lord will awaken the hearts of a generation to know Him again.

Great deliverance will sweep through the homosexual community, and those bound by any kind of sexual sin, substance abuse, mental or emotional addiction will become free. This season of the next four years cannot be a time of ease for the church as we must seek the Lord like never before to prepare ourselves for an influx of "less desirables" into the church. At the same time, we must get ready for what will happen on a national scale as the hand of God moves across the nation in simultaneous judgment and revival.

One night after fifteen years of pastoring in my city and region, I received a prophetic dream. I was in a very large, three-story house. I had to get to the third level because the person I needed to speak with was on the third floor. I kept searching for a stairway or elevator but there was none to be found. As I walked around looking for the way up, there were others on the same level who were disrespectful to me. One man kept hitting me with a switch. Most old-fashioned switches are made of wood, but this one was made of metal. Every time he walked by, he "switched me." I finally decided to find out where this man was from. As a pastor, I figured this person had been hurt at a prior church or somewhere in life, and that was the reason he was trying to hurt me.

I approached him in the dream and asked, "How long have you been here?" I thought if I could get some information, I would be able to help him. He said, "Three thousand years!" Suddenly, his face twisted. I began to rebuke him in Jesus' name, realizing I wasn't dealing with a man but a demonic entity. Then I woke up. I knew I had had a divine encounter. Every personal, financial, and ministry "switch" that I had personally experienced was not just life's normal occurrences but had been a spiritual attack. Demons inhabited the world long before people. God showed me there was a 3,000-year-old entity that had staked its claim over my area and now felt threatened because we were having regular awakening prayer meetings, calling out to the Lord for real revival. I told my church that following Sunday that many of the issues they were struggling with were not just everyday life's coincidences but the result of a spiritual being attempting to keep them from complete freedom in Christ.

America is being "switched" by unseen entities, and some of you reading this right now have been dealing with personal, family, business, and church issues and can't understand why there isn't a change or breakthrough. You have been caught up in political arguments and the friction of a nation that has drifted away from the Lord. Put your gaze a little higher to the One who holds all victory in His hand.

God is standing at the door! Use His weapons and declare that *"greater is he who is in you than he who is in this world!"* Your breakthrough into an Elijah anointing to affect the nation with the power and presence of God is coming in Jesus' name!

Chapter 2
Stop the Party

The Bible says Elijah suddenly appeared in the court of King Ahab and his wife, Jezebel. Elijah's word to the leadership of the nation stated that for the next three and a half years, there would be no rain, not even dew, in the entire nation. Just think about an unknown man addressing the ruler, leader, king, president, or prime minister and telling them he had a word directly from God. I can imagine the cynicism of the entire administration of Ahab and the laughter after Elijah exited the palace. All the e-mail and social media accounts lit up to make fun of this religious relic—until it stopped raining.

In any society, especially one built on agriculture, consider how devastating a lack of moisture over an extended period of time would be and what would take place in the nation if that were to happen. It would not only be an economic disaster, but it would result in the death of thousands of people and animals. Why would God bring such a severe judgment on the land?

Ahab and specifically Jezebel had turned the nation over to Baal worship and had made it the state religion. Baal was considered the god of weather and fertility. According to Dennis Bratcher of the Christian Research Institute:

> Ba'al was the storm god, the bringer of rain, and thus fertility, to the land. There was rivalry among the gods and a struggle erupted between Yamm, the sea, and Ba'al, the rain. With the help of his

sister Anat, the goddess of war, and Astarte, the goddess of earth and fertility, Ba'al defeated Yamm, and his cohorts, Tannin, the dragon of the sea, and Loran (or Lothan, cf. Isaiah 27:1), the serpent with seven heads. The gods began to build a magnificent house for Ba'al so that he could be at rest and provide abundant rain for the earth. But Ba'al was challenged by Mot (or Mut), the god of death and the underworld. Mot temporarily triumphed and Ba'al disappeared into the underworld. Anat and Shapash, the sun god, found Ba'al, brought him back to life, and restored him to his house.[3] The disappearance of rain in the dry season (Ba'al's descent into the underworld) portended catastrophe if it did not return in the Spring.

It was also believed the hot summers were a result of Baal's displeasure, and Baal had to be resurrected from the dead every year from the nether world. Baal could be appeased through sexual immorality, heterosexual and homosexual; child sacrifice; and pantheism, or worship of the environment at the expense of people and their needs.

This immoral activity resulted in unwanted pregnancies, but that wasn't a problem as Baal would accept children as a sacrifice. Huge fires were started in the lap of Baal and the child would be placed in the arms of this idol. Drums played as a way to drown out the screams of the child so the parent would not hear the baby and potentially remove the child from the altar. Israel practiced this ritual in many forms with different gods named Molech, Chemosh, and others, but they were all forms of Baal worship.

The problem was not just that everyone had turned themselves over to Baal. The greater issue was that they worshiped Baal and attempted to worship God at the same time. Lest we think this doesn't have any relevance to us today, you may remember that in the spring of 2016, a number of news media ran an article about the "arch of

---

3. Dennis Bratcher. "Ba'al Worship in the Old Testament." Copyright © 2016 CRI/Voice, Institute, Accessed December 27, 2016. http://www.crivoice.org/baal.html.

Baal" to be constructed for display in New York City and in London, where it stayed for one week before going on to Dubai. The company constructing the arches plans to build thousands of them around the world. Their rationale is to show their defiance toward ISIS as ISIS has destroyed the original temples.

> **Legalized sexual immorality, abortion, and pantheistic perspectives cloaked as environmentalism has been packaged under a new name called progressivism.**

We are presently surrounded by Baal worship in America as the desire to feel a temporary pleasure trumps morality. Because truth is relative and we no longer have a standard on which to base right and wrong, we are doing what is right in our own eyes. Legalized sexual immorality, abortion, and pantheistic perspectives cloaked as environmentalism, or climate change, has been packaged under a new name called progressivism. In Romans 1, Paul referred to this as worshiping the creation instead of the Creator.

> *So they worshiped and served the things God created instead of the Creator himself* (Romans 1:25).

Anyone who considers themselves a political progressive is repeating the same mistake Israel made in ancient times and will reap the same detrimental consequences. Consider that the average tax payer in America pays approximately $8,500.00 a year in taxes.[4] Since 1973, we have taken the lives of nearly 60 million babies through abortion. If you just take twenty-five years, those lives over time would have paid over twelve trillion dollars into the national

---

4. Todd Campbell, "The Average American Pays This Much in Income Taxes—How Do You Compare?" The Motley Fool, January 31, 2015, accessed December 27, 2016, http://www.fool.com/investing/general/2015/01/31/the-average-american-pays-this-much-in-income-taxe.aspx.

treasury. Considering our national debt, America has murdered itself into its present debt crisis. Those who support a women's right to choose need to consider their contribution to the financial collapse of America.

It's hard to imagine we have now legalized same-sex marriage. But there is an underlying issue in this that goes beyond the act of homosexual sex. Both the Talmud and Midrash, Jewish rabbinical literature, contain oral traditions, exegesis of Torah texts, and homiletic stories that give us insight into Jewish and biblical history.

One of the teachings refers to the judges of Sodom (Genesis 19), who historically were named Kaz-sheker (greatest liar), Rab-sheker (master of lies), Rab-nabel, (master of turpitude), Rab-masteh Din (chief perverter of the law), and Kelepandar (forger). These judges had enforced laws that were sexually permissive and oppressive to the poor, which resulted in a society where justice and legal sense were ignored to accommodate the desires of a ruling few. This resulted in a chaotic culture, which historical and biblical accounts record as an "upside-down" civilization with the weak exploited by the rich and powerful.

One story tells of a poor man who was secretly kept alive with scraps of bread by a compassionate citizen. When the judges found out, they ruled this gracious person be burnt to death.[5] It's hard for us to imagine such a thing, and yet that was how Sodom and the cities of the plain lived each day. In addition, the biblical record tells us that Lot, Abraham's nephew, was daily tormented with the filthy conversation and lifestyle of the wicked people around him (2 Peter 2:8).

---

5. In Sodom, everyone who gave bread and water to the poor was condemned to death by fire (Yalḳ., Gen. 83). Two girls, one poor and the other rich, went to a well; and the former gave the latter her jug of water, receiving in return a vessel containing bread. When this became known, both were burned alive. Joseph Jacobs and Schulim Ochser. "JewishEncyclopedia.com," Sodom, 2011, accessed December 27, 2016, http://www. jewishencyclopedia.com/articles/13827-sodom. Public domain.

Stop the Party

The Genesis record tells us that God heard the cries of those who were oppressed and went down to deal with the wickedness of Sodom (Genesis 19:20-21). On the fateful night, a homosexual mob of men gathered outside of Lot's house and demanded he open the door so the men could have sex with the visitors staying at Lot's home. These were the angels God had sent to rescue Lot, but the mob did not know this.

Those who say the sin of Sodom had nothing to do with homosexuality and sexual looseness ignore the clear account of the Genesis text, the 2 Peter text, and Jude 7 that refers to gross immorality in Sodom. In addition, the prophet Ezekiel expands on this and gives us a comprehensive view of Sodom and the culture of the cities of the plain: *"Behold, this was the guilt of your sister Sodom: she and her daughters had arrogance, abundant food and careless ease, but she did not help the poor and needy. Thus they were haughty and committed abominations before Me"* (Ezekiel 16:49-50 NASB). Their overabundance and careless ease led to abominations referred to as sexual perversion.

As a result of the rulings of a few judges who felt it was a civil duty to impose their personal views on the entire population, justice and morality had been denied in every area of Sodom's culture. People in Sodom had no choice but to agree, be silent, leave, or, if they spoke up, risk their futures and very life.

It continually amazes me how relevant and up-to-date the Bible is in the twenty-first century. Activist judges in America are daily overruling the will of the people and imposing immoral, personal views on the citizens of this country on a number of issues, distorting justice at every turn. Many states have wrongly had the imposition of the minority forced on the majority as laws are set aside through dishonest, judicial tyranny.

It was the rulings of the judges of Sodom that brought the judgment of God on Sodom and the cities of the plain, and following

The Elijahs of God

the historical pattern it will be the rulings of activist judges and a silent, sleepy Christian majority that will result in the swift hand of judgment on America too.

In *Sex and Culture* (1934), J.D. Unwin (a British ethnologist and social anthropologist at Oxford University and Cambridge University) studied eighty primitive tribes and six known civilizations through 5,000 years of history and found a positive correlation between the cultural achievement of a people and the sexual restraint they observed.[6] "*Sex and Culture* is a work of the highest importance," said Aldous Huxley. He wrote:

> Unwin's conclusions, which are based upon an enormous wealth of carefully sifted evidence, may be summed up as follows. All human societies are in one or another of four cultural conditions: zoistic, manistic, deistic, rationalistic. Of these societies the zoistic displays the least amount of mental and social energy, the rationalistic the most. Investigation shows that the societies exhibiting the least amount of energy are those where prenuptial continence is not imposed and where the opportunities for sexual indulgence after marriage are greatest. The cultural condition of a society rises in exact proportion as it imposes pre-nuptial and post-nuptial restraints upon sexual opportunity.[7]

According to Unwin, after a nation becomes prosperous it becomes increasingly liberal with regard to sexual morality and as a result "loses its cohesion, its impetus, and its purpose."[8] The process, says the author, is irreversible:

> The whole of human history does not contain a single instance of a group becoming civilized unless it has been absolutely

6. J.D. Unwin, *Sex and Culture*, (London: Oxford University Press), p. 412.
7. Aldous Huxley, "Ethics," *Ends and Means*, (London: Chatto & Windus, 1946), p. 311–12.
8. J.D. Unwin, *Sex and Culture*, (London: Oxford University Press), p. 412.

monogamous, nor is there any example of a group retaining its culture after it has adopted less rigorous customs.[9]

Any human society is free to choose either to display great energy or to enjoy sexual freedom; the evidence is that it cannot do both for more than one generation.[10]

> **Any human society is free to choose either to display great energy or to enjoy sexual freedom; the evidence is that it cannot do both for more than one generation.**

Stop the Party

Remember, I am not being "sin specific" and ignoring the many other sins of our culture or the body of Christ, which range from gluttony to gossip. There are many things grieving the heart of God, especially a church culture that has compromised and is now syncretistic in their worship of multiple gods with Jesus being one of the many. The prophet Isaiah gives us a striking account of this attitude in God's people.

Isaiah 22 contrasts a sleeping, pleasure-ridden, religious culture with a weeping prophet trying to get Israel's attention. The Assyrian army had conquered many cities in Judah and had surrounded Jerusalem. Isaiah asked why God's people were gathering on the rooftops to party, confident of their victory, when they had not called on the name of the Lord. Listen to the description Isaiah gives:

> *What is happening? Why is everyone running to the rooftops? The whole city is in a terrible uproar. What do I see in this reveling city? Bodies are lying*

9. J. D. Unwin, "Monogamy as a Condition of Social Energy," The Hibbert Journal, 1927, Vol. XXV, p. 662

10. J.D. Unwin, *Sex and Culture*, (London: Oxford University Press), p. 412.

everywhere, killed not in battle but by famine and disease.... Chariots fill your beautiful valleys, and charioteers storm your gates. Judah's defenses have been stripped away. You run to the armory for your weapons. You inspect the breaks in the walls of Jerusalem. You store up water in the lower pool. You survey the houses and tear some down for stone to strengthen the walls. Between the city walls, you build a reservoir for water from the old pool. But you never ask for help from the One who did all this. You never considered the One who planned this long ago.

At that time the Lord, the Lord of Heaven's Armies, called you to weep and mourn. He told you to shave your heads in sorrow for your sins and to wear clothes of burlap to show your remorse. But instead, you dance and play; you slaughter cattle and kill sheep. You feast on meat and drink wine. You say, "Let's feast and drink, for tomorrow we die!" (Isaiah 22:1-2,7-13)

It is striking that even though they saw an approaching enemy, the danger to the city and its people, Israel continued to ignore the obvious and loved pleasure more than their God.

The church finds itself in the same place again in the twenty-first century. Nations are in turmoil, culture is becoming more antichrist, debt continues to climb, and 80 percent of American churches have plateaued or are in decline.[11] One would think church members and leaders would be running through the streets with their hair on fire, trying to get people's attention. That is not the case.

We continue to be content with church as usual. We absent ourselves from corporate prayer meetings because we are too busy

11. Aubrey Malphurs, "The State of the American Church: Plateaued or Declining," TMG Blog, September 5, 2014, accessed December 28, 2016, http://www.malphursgroup.com/state-of-the-american-church-plateaued-declining/.

with our plans instead of God's. We live for our vacations, alcohol, and drugs and think God doesn't care. We date while separated from our spouses, commit adultery, seldom read God's Word, and look just like the world we are supposed to be separated from. We have no power to raise the dead because we are dead ourselves and don't realize we are living in a backslidden condition.

> **There is a wake-up call coming to America and the American church. The next eighteen months will bring radical shifts to our way of life and how we perceive our role in the world.**

National, regional, and local church leaders appear more interested in their corporate meeting agendas than seeking the face of God. Seldom is there a discussion about the need for personal and national awakening; and those who do speak about it are looked at as odd aberrations from the accepted modern church cultural model. And all the while we are losing the next generation to a secular society because the church has now become secular in practice and has no power to get between the living and the dead.

We seem so spiritually confident, yet Isaiah closed this chapter with these words:

> *But the Lord of Heaven's Armies also says: "The time will come when I will pull out the nail that seemed so firm. It will come out and fall to the ground. Everything it supports will fall with it. I, the Lord, have spoken!"*
> (Isaiah 22:25)

There is a wake-up call coming to America and the American church. The next eighteen months will bring radical shifts to our way of life and how we perceive our role in the world. God tells us that every part of society will be affected:

The Elijahs of God

> *Look! The Lord is about to destroy the earth and make it a vast wasteland. He devastates the surface of the earth and scatters the people. Priests and laypeople, servants and masters, maids and mistresses, buyers and sellers, lenders and borrowers, bankers and debtors—none will be spared* (Isaiah 24:1-2).

Yet the Lord never leaves us without hope! Even though Israel refused, God's desire is still for us to turn back to Him:

> *At that time the Lord, the Lord of Heaven's Armies, called you to weep and mourn. He told you to shave your heads in sorrow for your sins and to wear clothes of burlap to show your remorse* (Isaiah 22:12).

> *In that day, everyone in the land of Judah will sing this song: Our city is strong! We are surrounded by the walls of God's salvation. Open the gates to all who are righteous; allow the faithful to enter. You will keep in perfect peace all who trust in you, all whose thoughts are fixed on you! Trust in the Lord always, for the Lord God is the eternal Rock. He humbles the proud and brings down the arrogant city. He brings it down to the dust. The poor and oppressed trample it underfoot, and the needy walk all over it. But for those who are righteous, the way is not steep and rough. You are a God who does what is right, and you smooth out the path ahead of them. Lord, we show our trust in you by obeying your laws; our heart's desire is to glorify your name. All night long I search for you; in the morning I earnestly seek for God. For only when you come to judge the earth will people learn what is right* (Isaiah 26:1-9).

It's not too late for us! It's not too late for the church or America, and this is where the Elijahs of God enter the stage of a nation!

Remember that God will never allow the spirit of the world to control anything without the spirit of God confronting it. The spirit of Elijah is going to enter those who are hungry for God in order to confront the spirit of Baal in the church and the government. What is getting ready to happen in America is unprecedented. As great as past awakenings have been, the next move of God will overwhelm this nation as the fire of God burns up what is false and the power of God brings back the rain. God is going to empower you! God walked Elijah through a process, and God will take us through the same journey if we desire to be a force of change in our nation. Get ready—you're going to have a radical life shift!

Chapter 3
Are You There?

W e all want to experience the fire and rain from heaven, but God could not get Elijah to that place until He walked him through the steps of personal awakening. Elijah went through a learning curve that must happen with all of us.

The Learning Curve of Extreme Peace

The Bible says, *"The word of the Lord came to Elijah: 'Leave here, turn eastward and hide in the Kerith Ravine, east of the Jordan'"* (1 Kings 17:2-3 NIV).

There were many of these unknown places in the rocks, so if he went there, they wouldn't be able to find Elijah.

> *You will drink from the brook, and I have directed the ravens to supply you with food there* (1 Kings 17:4 NIV).

This was a specific place. *I want you to go there.* Elijah is in the wilderness, by himself, with the ravens bringing him breakfast and supper, and he can drink from the brook all day long. Wouldn't life be great like that all the time? Someone might think this sure is a lazy Christian! Let's understand what God is trying to teach Elijah: his culture was in chaos. There was no rain. Crops weren't growing, people were rioting and stealing what little food there was and national leaders had walked away from God. The lack of water caused fires to break out that destroyed vast areas of land

The Elijahs of God

and buildings. Where was Elijah? He was sitting in the middle of perfect peace, unaffected by the rest of the nation's mayhem.

What God wants us to grasp is that the culture around us does not need to affect the peace that is within us. When everything is bedlam around you, God's intent is that there is peace within you. The reality is that most of us are affected internally by what happens externally when it's supposed to be the reverse—what happens externally is supposed to be influenced by the presence of Jesus inside of us. Whatever is going on around you in your home, your life, your family is a direct result of what's taking place within you. All of us carry an attitude or spirit that affects our external world. A lack of peace externally only reveals what's really going on in the core of our being.

> **All personal peace comes out of the secret place. If I'm not in the secret place with God *internally*, then there will be no peace with anything *externally*.**

Israel walked in the wilderness for forty years, but long before that even began they'd already wandered away from God in their hearts. Walking in the wilderness became an external manifestation of what had already taken place internally. External peace is not about what goes on around you; external peace is dictated by what goes on within you. Let me put it like this: If your home is always in chaos, it's not because of what other people are doing. It's because of what is happening within you. The external is only a reflection of the internal.

God was trying to help Elijah understand that if you've got peace within, it doesn't matter what takes place without. This is what's known as the secret place with God. All personal peace comes out of the secret place. If I'm not in the secret place with God *internally*, then there will be no peace with anything *externally*. God is trying to help Elijah grasp the key to his own peace. There are many people who don't have calm on the inside because they have no private peace. Before we can have public victory, we have to have private peace. Before this man can lead a

44

chaotic nation back to peace with God, he must know peace himself. Are you there?

David said:

> *Whoever dwells in the shelter of the Most High will rest in the shadow of the Almighty. I will say of the Lord, "He is my refuge and my fortress, my God, in whom I trust"* (Psalms 91:1-2 NIV).

We must get to the secret place where nothing external has the ability to affect what's going on in our life before we can lead a nation back to end-time revival.

The Learning Curve of Extreme Provision

This is important. Elijah's nation was struggling to survive.

> *Some time later the brook dried up because there had been no rain in the land. Then the word of the Lord came to him* (1 Kings 17:7-8 NIV).

When you think about changing jobs, making big life decisions, moving, selling your house, or even changing a church, do you consider the will of God? The first question most people ask is, "How will this benefit me? The question they should ask is, "Where does God want me?" That's the only place of provision. There are some people who consistently struggle because they have not put themselves in the place where God told them to be. They are running after everything else instead of the will of God.

When provision for Elijah ran out, he did not stay there because it was more convenient or familiar. God told him He was going to send him somewhere else, so he had to *go there*. What would've happened if Elijah had stayed at the brook? He would have died. God says, "I've got you covered. G*o there* as I've directed a widow to care for you." Widows in that day had nothing. God said, "I'm going to provide for you where there

The Elijahs of God

is nothing." Can I say that to you again? God says, "I'm going to provide for you where there is nothing, so go to the widow. She'll supply you with food." Elijah went to Zerapheth, and when he came to the town gate a widow was gathering sticks. He asked her to get him some water and a piece of bread.

That might not seem like a big deal, but when you don't have anything, a piece of bread is a lot. For some people a hundred dollars might as well be a million because they have nothing. She said to him:

> *I swear by the Lord your God that I don't have a single piece of bread in the house. And I have only a handful of flour left in the jar and a little cooking oil in the bottom of the jug. I was just gathering a few sticks to cook this last meal, and then my son and I will die* (1 Kings 17:12).

For her, life was over and Elijah *arrogantly* said, "Don't be afraid!" Any time the Bible says *don't be afraid*, there's a reason to fear! That's why God tells us not to be afraid. Tell yourself: "I will not be afraid!" Depending on the translation, some count 365 "don't be afraids" in the Bible—one for each day of the year! Elijah said, "Don't be afraid. Go home, make a small loaf of bread for me with what you have and bring it, then make something for yourself and your son." The widow was wondering: *I don't have enough for myself and my son; how will there be enough for you?* Then God got involved:

> *For this is what the Lord, the God of Israel, says: "The jar of flour will not be used up and the jug of oil will not run dry until the day the Lord sends rain on the land." She went away and did as Elijah had told her. So there was food every day for Elijah and the woman and her family. For the jar of flour was not used up and the jug of oil did not run dry, in keeping with the word of the Lord spoken by Elijah* (1 Kings 17:14-16 NIV).

When we planted the church we are pastoring, there were very few resources. Those were the days before church planting organizations and partner ministries had resources to give and get behind a new ministry. Driving one day, I turned to my wife and said, "How are we going to do this?" She replied, "We are going to trust God!" What an obvious answer, one I needed to hear! While ministering the following Sunday, Bethel Church in Blackwood, New Jersey handed us a check for $10,000 and placed confidence in the call of God we had sensed. Even though it would take additional money, that first seed provided the faith to believe God for many more financial miracles.

Let me ask you a question. Are you there? Can you believe God for extreme provision? You say, "I don't have anything." When you have nothing, whose obligation is it to provide? You've tried; you've worked at it. It hasn't happened. God is teaching the Elijahs of God that He will bring extreme peace and extreme provision when everything around us is in chaos!

The Learning Curve of Extreme Power

Sometime later, the son of the woman who owned the house became ill, he grew worse and worse and finally stopped breathing. She said to Elijah, what do you have against me, man of God? Did you come to remind me of my sin and kill my son? (1 Kings 17:17-18 NIV)

Let's pause right here. Isn't it interesting that when people are living with the guilt of their past they think everything bad that happens to them is God's judgment? This bad thing happened because I did this or that. How many of you have ever had the fleeting thought in your mind, *Maybe this is God punishing me?* Stop that thinking now! If God planned to punish her, why did He bother to provide for her and the boy? Sometimes our guilt becomes so overwhelming that we can't see past our own shame. If God was punishing you, this book of encouragement would never have reached your hands!

47

The Elijahs of God

Elijah took the child in his arms, went to an upper room, his secret place, and called on the name of the Lord. He said, *"Lord my God, have you brought tragedy even on this widow I am staying with, by causing her son to die?"* (1 Kings 17:20 NIV). The answer was no. Then Elijah stretched himself out on the boy multiple times. He laid on the boy face to face, hand to hand, eyes to eyes. He imparted vision, breath, and life. He declared the boy was to speak and do the work of God!

Some of you need to lay on dead hopes and dreams, and instead of imparting your own discouragement, shame, and struggle, declare that what is dead will live! Many of us have talked about our dreams for years, but we've never said anything positive and we've lost hope. As Elijah stretched himself out, the boy's life returned to him. The Lord heard Elijah's cry, and He will hear your cry! This kind of extreme power is the only thing that can turn our nation back to God.

When the apostle Paul began his ministry in Corinth, he realized it would take more than sermons and songs to make an inroad into the Corinthian culture. Corinth was so vile that people had coined the phrase "to corithianize" to refer to the debauchery of the people. Paul made it clear that his only hope of success was supernatural power.

> *When I first came to you, dear brothers and sisters, I didn't use lofty words and impressive wisdom to tell you God's secret plan. For I decided that while I was with you I would forget everything except Jesus Christ, the one who was crucified. I came to you in weakness— timid and trembling. And my message and my preaching were very plain. Rather than using clever and persuasive speeches, I relied only on the power of the Holy Spirit. I did this so you would trust not in human wisdom but in the power of God* (1 Corinthians 2:1-5).

In his book *Hunger Driven*, Brian Nickens calls for us to desire more than Sunday morning church as usual. He states:

If our intellectual pursuit of Bible knowledge does not lead us into experiences equivalent to those we read about in Scripture, we become a spawning ground for the spirit of religion and a playground for demons. The demonic realm knows that churches and ministries who pride themselves in doctrinal purity and their supposedly solid, biblical foundations tend to be powerless when it comes to ousting spiritual forces from their midst, so the demons settle in…. If you desire a Christian experience that continually increases in anointing, power, victory and supernatural manifestations then you must ditch all preconceived notions about what God can and cannot do…. Even Jesus deferred to the miraculous works as the proof to validate His identity: "If I don't do the works of my Father, don't believe me. But if I do them, though you don't believe me, believe the works; that you may know and believe that the Father is in me." John 10:38-39.[12]

> **If our intellectual pursuit of Bible knowledge does not lead us into experiences equivalent to those we read about in Scripture, we become a spawning ground for the spirit of religion and a playground for demons.**

Aren't you tired of showy platform worship that draws attention to the worshiper instead of Jesus? Don't you long for ministry that causes a room to rush to an altar instead of motivational speaking that makes people feel comfortable in their sin and results in no life change? The supernatural gifts of the Holy Spirit did not cease with the first century church, and God is going to empower modern day Elijahs to impact this country and reveal the truth of Jesus! Lay before the Lord and call on His name for the life of God to enter this nation again! He lives, and the nation can live again too!

---

12. Brian Nickens, Hunger Driven: Overcoming Fear and Skepticism of the Supernatural Christian Lifestyle, CreateSpace Independent Publishing Platform, 2015, Kindle Edition.

Chapter 4
It's Not Over

I t was in 1926 when Watchman Nee, the great Chinese preacher, took a group of individuals to a small town in China to share the gospel. Watchman Nee was an amazing Bible teacher and theologian and wrote many books. He would spend the last twenty years of his life in prison for his faith as communism rose in China and authorities didn't want him teaching Christian principles any longer. As they began ministering in the village, it seemed no one was interested in what they had to say and did not want any of their literature. The people were kind, but as they started to speak of Jesus villagers sort of mumbled something and then walked away. As they gathered in the evening, each team member had experienced the same response.

The next day they went out again to sell their Bibles and share Christ. One young man was newly saved. He got so frustrated at the lack of response that he publicly asked, "Why will you not respond to us?" They told him they did not need Jesus along with the rest of the gods they already had. Besides that, they were getting ready to celebrate the Festival of Ta-Wang, their local god, whose name meant "a great king." For 286 years they had celebrated this festival and it had never rained on that day. The young man was so frustrated he just blurted out, "It's going to rain on the eleventh and there will be no festival!" This soon spread throughout the community of 20,000 that a young preacher said there was going to be rain on the eleventh and there would be no Ta-Wang Festival.

The Elijahs of God

When they got back to their lodgings, Watchman realized this was a serious problem. Up to this point they had been afraid to pray for rain. Suddenly, a flash of inspiration came to Watchman's mind: "Where is the Lord God of Elijah?" They took this as a word from the Lord and began to believe for rain on the eleventh just as the man had said. They prayed and prayed until God gave them peace, but when they went back out the next day there was still no response from the villagers. However, this time the people said if it rained on Ta-Wang day, Jesus is God and if it didn't, Ta-Wang is God.

They woke up on the morning of the eleventh, and it was a sunny day. As they ate breakfast they suddenly heard raindrops begin to drop on the top of the house. They prayed and asked God for a downpour. Before long, it was raining so hard that the streets were beginning to flood. The townspeople tried to bring the idol out, but there was so much mud they tripped and fell and broke its jaw and left arm. The teenagers of that community started to say Ta-Wang was no god!

It rained for two hours, from nine in the morning to eleven. Tradition said they could not postpone the celebration for more than an hour, so they had to take Ta-Wang back in and couldn't have the festival. The people that ran the festival said Ta-Wang didn't really intend to come out today. He intended to come on the evening of the fourteenth instead. So Watchmen's team prayed and asked God to let it rain on the evening of the fourteenth too. Before they were to bring Ta-Wang out, it poured so hard that they couldn't even get the idol out the door. The team began to share the truth about Jesus, and the power of God moved in the community because God showed who was God.[13]

The future of that community rested in the hands of one young man who was willing to believe God for something that had never taken place in over 200 years. What's that got to do with us today?

---

13. Watchman Nee, *Sit, Walk, Stand* (Fort Washington, PA: Christian Literature Crusade, 1962).

Remember that Elijah gave a word that there would be no rain or dew for over three years. At that moment, the future of Israel no longer rested in the hands of Ahab and Jezebel; it rested in the hand of one prophet who heard from God and said this is what's going to take place. God had to be this forceful because Ahab had refused to follow the pattern for a new king. The Mosaic Law required a king at his coronation to be given a copy of the law. It was his responsibility to learn it, study it, obey it, meditate on it, and help the nation live by it.

You are about to enter the land the Lord your God is giving you. When you take it over and settle there, you may think, "We should select a king to rule over us like the other nations around us." If this happens, be sure to select as king the man the Lord your God chooses. You must appoint a fellow Israelite; he may not be a foreigner.

The king must not build up a large stable of horses for himself or send his people to Egypt to buy horses, for the Lord has told you, "You must never return to Egypt." The king must not take many wives for himself, because they will turn his heart away from the Lord. And he must not accumulate large amounts of wealth in silver and gold for himself.

When he sits on the throne as king, he must copy for himself this body of instruction on a scroll in the presence of the Levitical priests. He must always keep that copy with him and read it daily as long as he lives. That way he will learn to fear the Lord his God by obeying all the terms of these instructions and decrees. This regular reading will prevent him from becoming proud and acting as if he is above his fellow citizens. It will also prevent him from turning away from these commands in the smallest way. And it will ensure that he and his descendants will reign for many generations in Israel (Deuteronomy 17:14-20).

The Elijahs of God

Priests and prophets assisted the kings in implementing the Law, and the kings made sure the Law was obeyed throughout the land. But as the kings began to drift away from God, eventually the kings or government were on one side and the prophets or local ministry and churches on the other. There was no more agreement between the two about how God had founded the nation. God had to get the attention of the nation. To do that, He gave a clear word to His chosen vessel, the prophet, that would affect everyone and everything in the nation. Is it possible that God is clearly speaking His words to America through many known and unknown prophetic voices today? Absolutely! Every believer has the capability to hear from the Lord and speak His words in their local context.

Revelation 19:10 states, *"The essence of prophecy is to give a clear witness for Jesus."*

In the same way Elijah's words became reality to the entire nation, the words you speak every day become a prophetic word from God to the circumstances, situations, the church, and ultimately the nation that you are living in. God told them there will be no rain for three and a half years. Initially, that sounds punitive and uncaring, like a punishment from a judgmental God. That opinion of God fails to understand His long-term purpose for humanity.

At that moment, no one could see that it was God's ultimate purpose to bring rain. A myopic vision of God fails to understand that all of God's acts toward us are redemptive, not punitive. God loves His creation so much that when we drift away from Him, He gets our attention. Many of us can personally testify to this if we've ever been in a backslidden condition. Unexpected difficulties begin to happen. He isn't judging us though. He is simply using circumstances to get our attention. At the time, we might have thought that what was taking place was going to tear us apart. We couldn't see it was the redeeming power of God. We didn't understand that He was pulling us back so we didn't get so far away that we'd never return.

54

This is what David meant in Psalms 119:67 (NIV) when he said, *"Before I was afflicted I went astray, but now I obey your word."* The writer to the Hebrews reminds us:

> *And have you forgotten the encouraging words God spoke to you as his children? He said, "My child, don't make light of the Lord's discipline, and don't give up when he corrects you. For the Lord disciplines those he loves, and he punishes each one he accepts as his child."*
>
> *As you endure this divine discipline, remember that God is treating you as his own children. Who ever heard of a child who is never disciplined by its father? If God doesn't discipline you as he does all of his children, it means that you are illegitimate and are not really his children at all. Since we respected our earthly fathers who disciplined us, shouldn't we submit even more to the discipline of the Father of our spirits, and live forever?*
>
> *For our earthly fathers disciplined us for a few years, doing the best they knew how. But God's discipline is always good for us, so that we might share in his holiness. No discipline is enjoyable while it is happening—it's painful! But afterward, there will be a peaceful harvest of right living for those who are trained in this way* (Hebrews 12:5-11).

God does this with us individually and nationally. He declares His intent, through His servants, to make a bold declaration about His will for a country. Just as the future of Israel rested in the hands of one obedient prophet, so the future of America rests in the hands of an obedient church. The future of this republic is in our hands!

> *At times I might shut up the heavens so that no rain falls, or command grasshoppers to devour your crops, or send plagues among you. Then if my people who are called by*

my name will humble themselves and pray and seek my face and turn from their wicked ways, I will hear from heaven and will forgive their sins and restore their land (2 Chronicles 7:13-14).

Hallelujah! This nation can be restored and healed! What are the evidences that God is dealing with a nation? There are certain markers to look for that are historical and biblical proofs that God is at work.

God will grant economic prosperity and blessing.

Because the goodness of God leads us to repentance (Romans 2:4) and because God is a giver, He begins with kindness and blessing. No one can deny America has received an abundant blessing from heaven. America is a leader around the world in every category. This was His pattern with Israel. Deuteronomy 28 lists the blessings Israel could expect if they were obedient. At one time they were the most powerful nation on earth.

God will call people back to Himself by the words of the prophets.

When we drift away from the Lord, He uses many ways to get our attention. Don't be fooled by liberal media or larger ministries who seem soft on sin. There are still multiple churches and individuals calling people into a relationship with God. You're not alone; keep speaking.

God will affect the economy in the reverse.

Not only does Deuteronomy 28 list the promise of blessings for obedience but also the curses on the nation should they turn their back on God. After the reign of Ahab and Jezebel, history records, *"At about that time the Lord began to cut down the size of Israel's territory"* (2 Kings 10:32). Few people realized this was the work of God, not the result of poor political decisions or inept government. Since 1973 (the same year Roe vs. Wade was passed), one can follow the challenging financial losses America has endured. At the writing of this book, we are $20 trillion in debt. Even our buildings are no longer the tallest in the world, a clear sign that prosperity has shifted from America.

God will allow inexperienced and immature leaders to come to power.

Near the end of Israel's existence as a nation before the captivity, kings became puppet rulers who achieved power through murder, personal intrigue, or appointment by a foreign nation. None of these kings were God's choice. Those in power became a reflection of the character of the nation. Isaiah 3 depicts what happens when God is attempting to bring a nation to its knees:

> *I will make boys their leaders, and toddlers their rulers. People will oppress each other—man against man, neighbor against neighbor. Young people will insult their elders, and vulgar people will sneer at the honorable. ...Childish leaders oppress my people, and women rule over them. O my people, your leaders mislead you; they send you down the wrong road* (Isaiah 3:4-5, 12).

God will allow the borders of the nation to be breached.

By the time Sennacherib had invaded Judah under King Hezekiah's reign, the Assyrians had already taken forty-six strong cities of Judah and countless unwalled villages. Over 200,000 people had been taken captive and the nation's borders had essentially become unprotected and unwalled.[14] We are all aware of the challenges with America's borders. Without borders, there is no nation, and without boundaries in a relationship with God, there is no Christianity.

God will remove protection and allow foreign enemies to attack and dominate economically, spiritually, and militarily.

With terrorism and threats from dominant world nations on the rise, one can only wonder what is coming if America continues on its present track. No matter how powerful our military might be, God's Word makes it clear that, *"Unless the Lord watches over the city, the guards stand watch in vain"* (Psalms 127:1 NIV).

---

14. G. V. Smith. *The New American Commentary.* (Nashville: B & H Publishing Group, 2007). "Isaiah 1-39," 384.

The Elijahs of God

At this point, only one of two things can happen—either the nation repents and turns back to God for restoration or the nation and its people go into captivity.

It's God's Time

Someone recently met with me and said that it was over for America. Do you believe that? Are you only looking at the circumstances around you instead of the God above you? It's a mistake to declare what we are seeing instead of what God is saying. Have we forgotten the impact of the First and Second Great Awakenings in the eighteenth and nineteenth centuries? Have we failed to remember the Welsh Revival, the Hebrides Awakening, or the Azusa Street outpouring in the early part of the 1900s in Los Angeles? Are we going to ignore the many times in biblical and worldwide history when many thought the day of the move of God was over, only to see God show up in miraculous ways?

Elijah was one man and his prayers were powerful. James reminds us, *"Elijah was a human being, even as we are. He prayed earnestly that it would not rain, and it did not rain on the land for three and a half years. Again he prayed, and the heavens gave rain, and the earth produced its crops"* (James 5:17-18 NIV).

If God responded to the prayers of one man, what would happen if the many righteous people in this country began to consistently call on the Lord for nationwide spiritual awakening? *The Elijahs of God never lose hope but continue to declare the purpose of God for nations.*

Tell the Righteous It Shall Be Well with Them

A number of years ago, I was ministering in the mountains of North Carolina. The church was at the base of a mountain, but my accommodations were on a lake at a higher elevation. There was such a difference in the elevation that it actually snowed where I was staying but did not snow down at the base of the mountain. Those of you who know me understand my preference for warm weather. That doesn't include snow!

The house on the lake was beautiful, but because it was winter very few people were staying in the homes surrounding me. I have to admit, it was a bit creepy at night. My daughter said to me, "Daddy, do you know what happens at lake houses at night in the dark?" That did not help my phobia! As a matter of fact, each evening after church I checked the house to make sure I was the only one staying there! I know. Don't fear!

> **God is preparing His Elijahs in the secret place to pronounce His words to a Baal-worshiping culture and usher in a last day spiritual awakening.**

One evening I worked late into the early morning hours and did not retire until around four in the morning. Oddly, I had the sense that I should pray for provision for myself and the church I pastor. Somewhere between 4 and 8 a.m. I dreamt of a terrible flood. It came from the East Coast and made it all the way over to our location. I remember needing to quickly climb higher to escape the flood waters; but the higher I climbed, the higher the floods waters rose. The foundations beneath me were collapsing until there was nothing left of the church. Then I woke up.

As I was thinking about this dream and what to tell my church a few days later, my eyes fell upon a passage of Scripture in Isaiah 3. I was a little concerned because I knew the dream was from the Lord to warn us of something coming in the future. As I pondered what it might mean, the Lord quickened my heart to Isaiah 3:10. The prior verses are warnings to Israel, but verse ten says, *"Say to the righteous that it shall be well with them, for they shall eat the fruit of their doings"* (NKJV).

The Lord was showing me that no matter what happens, those who walk with the Lord are secure. If there was ever a time to prepare for a cultural shift, it is now. God is preparing His Elijahs in the secret place to pronounce His words to a Baal-worshiping culture and usher in a last day spiritual awakening. Tell the righteous, *"It shall be well with them!"*

Part 2:

The Elijahs of God are Not Afraid of a Holy Confrontation

Chapter 5
Who Is the Problem?

Where is God? Why hasn't He answered my prayers? Why is it taking so long for Him to respond to me? I've heard those questions many times and have even asked them myself. Most of us can take short spans of challenge. We can endure a few days, weeks, or even months of difficulty. But years? The biggest obstacle to faith is not doubt. It's time. Time wears our faith thin and we can eventually lose hope.

Three and a half years is a long time for a nation to endure the effect of no rain. It is even more significant that there is no record of a clear word from God during the drought. It's one thing to struggle economically but far more serious to be living in a nation when God has chosen to be silent. Following the word given to Ahab, God told Elijah to go hide. Now God says go *"show yourself."* There is coming a moment when those who have been in the secret place will be released from private to speak powerful words in public. Don't be discouraged if you have a spiritual fire burning within you and have no one to share it with. Your moment is coming and you will be released into powerful anointing with answered prayers to go along with it!

As the scene unfolds, we get additional insight into what was happening during the time of Elijah's absence. The famine had been so severe in Samaria, the capital city of the northern kingdom of Israel, that even the animals didn't have enough food to survive. Ahab consulted his chief of staff, Obadiah, and both of them went to look for some grazing land to keep the animals alive. Scripture makes it clear that Obadiah was a devout worshiper of the Lord. He was the one who secretly hid 100 of the Lord's prophets in a cave to keep them safe from Jezebel's fury. We will discuss the significance of the spirit of Jezebel in the next chapter. Suffice it to say that she was an evil political ruler who hated anything that was righteous or pure. She would do anything including murder to stamp out any influence of the God of Israel. First Kings reveals the character of Ahab and Jezebel:

> *There was never anyone like Ahab, who sold himself to do evil in the eyes of the Lord, urged on by Jezebel his wife. He behaved in the vilest manner by going after idols, like the Amorites the Lord drove out before Israel* (1 Kings 21:25-26 NIV).

It is noteworthy that even though Ahab had the position, Jezebel held the power. This was a husband and wife who worked together to promote evil in mafia-style politics. Be wary of husband and wife teams in the church or politics who promote themselves for the purpose of personal power, wealth, and influence.

No matter how wicked leaders may be, God always has someone in a place of influence to be used of the Lord. I'm sure when Obadiah took the position in Ahab's administration, he didn't realize how wicked Ahab and Jezebel were going to be. After they assumed the throne, it didn't take long to see what their real intent was. It was at this point that Obadiah had to make a decision. Would he go along with this corrupt government to save himself or continue to serve the Lord? As a bold man of God, he chose to let his influence speak for the Lord and understood how important this choice was when Jezebel began killing men and woman of God. You may find yourself in a job or position where you are surrounded by evil people who want you to compromise your convictions. You're in the right place! God is going to use you to make a difference where you are.

It was a shock to Obadiah when Elijah appeared to him. Obadiah feared for his life. It was clear to Obadiah that if he told Ahab of Elijah's appearance and then the prophet disappeared, he could lose his life. Ahab was a dangerous man, but Elijah was not afraid. It's true that *"the godly are as bold as lions"* (Proverbs 28:1).

Ahab attempted to blame the nation's problems on Elijah. He called him a troublemaker.

Elijah corrected that assertion and called Ahab the same because Ahab had abandoned the Lord's command and followed the baals. Only wicked people cause trouble. It's always the desire of the wicked to change the story so they can blame righteous people for the consequences of their sin.

Tolerance has become a key word among many who advocate the changing of various laws in America from sexuality to free speech and gun control. However, is it really about tolerance or is it something else? *Tolerance* can refer to the willingness to put up with someone else's opinion, even if it conflicts with one's personal belief.

> **The loudest preachers of tolerance are the most intolerant, which suggests that tolerance is a pseudo-word for something else—legitimization.**

If tolerance were the real goal, those who say we should respect each other's opinions should be the most tolerant, even if someone disagrees. The fact is, the loudest preachers of tolerance are the most intolerant, which suggests that tolerance is a pseudo-word for something else—legitimization.

If this were just about tolerance, there would be no need to pass new laws about sexual behavior. We could just all get along, even if we did not agree with each other. However, when it comes to human sexuality, television, movies, elections, school curriculum, and a host of other media are attempting to convince us that if the law or church teaching can change, any kind of sexual behavior can be legitimized and accepted in the culture. There is a very real attempt to teach the next generation that if someone disagrees, don't tolerate them—silence them.

The Elijahs of God

In the spring of 2013, an ad was placed in a major American newspaper pleading with the pope to change the church's teachings on gay marriage. The stated goal of some left-wing, activist organizations is to "get homosexuality off the sin list." My response is to ask if they were also attempting to get every other sin the Bible mentions off the sin list too, to which they have no legitimate answer. The desire of some to end "religion-based bigotry" ignores the numerous instances of gay-based bigotry that are seldom acknowledged.

Other anti-Christian, antichrist groups consistently misrepresent true Christianity, misinterpret the clear teachings of Scripture, and mislead the next generation into thinking they are youth advocates, when in fact their only advocacy is an angry political agenda. There are many youth looking for a way out of the gay/lesbian/transgender lifestyle and there is a way out. Many have been wounded and abused as children and have confused a false identity with a true identity of freedom in Christ.

Freedom, however, is not through organizations who want to use them as political pawns but through people who genuinely love them. We understand the hurts of people and do not intend to hurt them more. We want every issue and struggle to come through our doors because we believe Jesus can fix anything! We often say, "No perfect people are allowed at our church because it would ruin everything!" Any church checking the religious boxes of acceptance is missing the heart of God.

Our doors are open for anyone because the true church loves this generation and will walk with them through any struggle they have. We must not let someone tell them differently and that we are somehow intolerant. As real Christians, we are the only ones who understand the millennial crisis in America. The Elijahs of God refuse to be redefined by hack political and social institutions and will rise up with delivering power to rescue a generation.

There have been multiple of instances where the intolerance of certain people in public positions with regard to faith has been evident with a goal to blame believers for challenging social issues. We've seen evangelicals

66

labeled as extremists and governmental chaplains fired for praying in the name of Jesus. We've witnessed federal judges prohibit prayer at graduation events and elementary kids ordered to have psychiatric evaluations for drawing pictures of Jesus. We've been told that the Ten Commandments can no longer be displayed, that inspirational Bible verses in public places must be removed, and we are living in a culture where truth has become the new hate speech.

> **The Elijahs of God refuse to be redefined by hack political and social institutions and will rise up with delivering power to rescue a generation.**

One school in Burlington, New Jersey actually did a mock shooting where one of the shooters was portrayed as a right-wing fundamentalist, upset that their child was forbidden to pray at the school.

I've personally been involved in a controversy where a local public school was going to produce a play that promoted the virtues of homosexuality to students. Through our efforts, the principal was brave enough and had the moral courage to cancel the play as we didn't feel the taxpayers should need to pay for a political and social agenda in the public school system. That began a national attack on us and the principal—all because we took a stand for morality toward the next generation.

In a speech to a pro-abortion group in 2015, then presidential candidate Hillary Clinton stated:

> Rights have to exist in practice—not just on paper…Laws have to be backed up with resources and political will. And deep-seated cultural codes, religious beliefs and structural biases have to be changed.

Even though she lost the election, this kind of thinking has permeated religious and political leaders; Bibles were even banned from a Chillicothe Veteran Affairs Medical Center in Athens, Ohio after a veteran complained.

The Elijahs of God

"Our government is secular, and must remain secular," the unidentified veteran wrote.

I remind you that God's judgment did not come on Israel because of Elijah's obedience but because of Ahab and Jezebel's disobedience and that of a nation of Israelites who should have known better than to follow them. Judgment will not come on America because of godly Christians but because of those who deny His Word, choose to live in defiance of His commands, and who pass laws as though they were shaking a fist in the face of God. At this point, we have to ask ourselves, what are we to do? More importantly, what is God going to do?

It's Time for a Confrontation

Please understand. I'm not just advocating a political confrontation. As I mentioned earlier, many of the moral battles of the day are being fought on the political battlefield. What we have seen over the last several months in the election cycle and public response to it is a tug of war between light and darkness. I am suggesting it's time for a visible confrontation with unseen powers of darkness and a holy people who have been empowered for such a time as this, with an outcome that cannot be in doubt.

Elijah suggested a dueling worship service between the God of Israel and the 450 prophets of Baal and 400 prophets of Asherah, Baal's female counterpart, on the top of a mountain called Carmel. The large number of Baal prophets reveals the extent to which Baal was worshiped and how detrimental the leadership of Jezebel and Ahab had been on the nation. This location was agreeable to Ahab because Carmel was considered a high point, the sacred home where Baal was honored. This would give his prophets the advantage.

Have You Ever Felt Alone?

Eight hundred and fifty false prophets who are intent on your death might have seemed intimidating to Elijah. Why was he not afraid of this confrontation? Because he knew he stood on the solid ground of truth. Many of you reading this book work or live in spiritually hostile environments. You have been told to be quiet about your faith as you cannot risk losing your job or close relationships. We have to understand that the move to silence our faith beyond the four walls of a church is demonic in nature.

We need to use wisdom and honor those in authority while making the most of every opportunity the Lord gives us to speak about Him. There is a real move though to keep our faith private. Political candidates use this terminology during elections to avoid personal controversy. It subtlety implies that the rest of us should do so as well. A faith that is only private is no faith at all. Jesus hung openly naked on a cross for our sin. Anyone's faith that is only private becomes a traitor to the cause of Christ. We are reminded of the apostles' response when told to stop preaching in the name of Jesus:

> *So they called the apostles back in and commanded them never again to speak or teach in the name of Jesus. But Peter and John replied, "Do you think God wants us to obey you rather than him? We cannot stop telling about everything we have seen and heard"* (Acts 4:18-20).

Don't be intimidated by the spirit of Jezebel that wants to silence your voice for Christ. You can be empowered by the same spirit that God gave Elijah.

As everyone gathered together for this spectacular worship event, Elijah asked one simple question. It's the same question the Lord has been asking through the ages regarding our worldview. *"How long will you waver between two opinions?"* (1 Kings 18:21a NIV). How long are you going to sit on the fence? How long are you going to vacillate between two worldviews? *"If the Lord is God, follow him! But if Baal is God, then follow him!"* (1 Kings 18:21b).

The Elijahs of God

One of the greatest challenges of twenty-first century Christianity is this inability to make a complete, sold-out commitment to the lordship of Jesus. We have in our minds that the flesh and the Holy Spirit can cohabitate without consequence. Paul instructed us:

> *Let the Holy Spirit guide your lives. Then you won't be doing what your sinful nature craves. The sinful nature wants to do evil, which is just the opposite of what the Spirit wants. And the Spirit gives us desires that are the opposite of what the sinful nature desires. These two forces are constantly fighting each other, so you are not free to carry out your good intentions* (Galatians 5:16-17).

The consequences of such actions result in a person who is completely unstable. James tells us:

> *Do not waver, for a person with divided loyalty is as unsettled as a wave of the sea that is blown and tossed by the wind. Such people should not expect to receive anything from the Lord. Their loyalty is divided between God and the world, and they are unstable in everything they do* (James 1:6-8).

What is your response to this? Is your life characterized by clear boundaries that evidence your commitment to Jesus, or are you still on the fence? The response of those in Elijah's day was silence because they could not justify their hypocrisy. Perhaps it had been so long since they had seen anything supernatural that they doubted the ability of God to do anything.

Who Is the Problem?

In the late 1980s I was ministering in southern Maine in a series of meetings. As I stepped over the threshold of the prayer room that evening, the Holy Spirit spoke to me and said, *It's been so long since people in this church have seen a move of God, they doubt that it can happen.* I thought I would just add this thought to my message. As it turned out, that was the message. As I shared this word of knowledge, the Spirit of God suddenly moved across the congregation, and the power of the Lord put to rest any doubt that God was still who He claimed to be as salvations and healings began to manifest.

God was getting ready to show the entire nation His fire, and He was going to prove one more time He was Lord over the weather in spite of the claim of an idol named Baal. At this moment, Elijah did an interesting thing—he called a prayer meeting! What better way to find out who God is simply by the one who answers prayer! The specific request was fire from heaven. Baal was the god of weather and fire, so the request shouldn't be a problem. Baal would certainly hear the cries of his worshipers and respond accordingly. It hadn't rained in three and a half years, so this was a great opportunity for Baal to vindicate himself.

At first glance, the silliness of believing in Baal seems obvious. And yet this is the case for the majority of humanity. Paul reminds us that:

> *Satan, who is the god of this world, has blinded the minds of those who don't believe. They are unable to see the glorious light of the Good News. They don't understand this message about the glory of Christ, who is the exact likeness of God* (2 Corinthians 4:4).

Elijah requested two bulls for sacrifice in this prayer meeting—one for himself and one for the false prophets. They were to prepare it on an altar but without fire. The proof of who was really God would be the one who responded with real fire.

And so the service began. All morning long, the prophets of Baal attempted to get a response. After several hours, Elijah began to taunt them:

The Elijahs of God

About noontime Elijah began mocking them. "You'll have to shout louder," he scoffed, "for surely he is a god! Perhaps he is daydreaming, or is relieving himself. Or maybe he is away on a trip, or is asleep and needs to be wakened!" (1 Kings 18:27).

Baal worshipers believed he rode along with ships on the sea to protect the sailors, so it was possible he was out of town. Because there was no response from Baal, the worshipers became more intense.

So they shouted louder, and following their normal custom, they cut themselves with knives and swords until the blood gushed out. They raved all afternoon until the time of the evening sacrifice, but still there was no sound, no reply, no response (1 Kings 18:28-29).

It was customary for Baal worshipers to mutilate their bodies during religious rites. However, this practice did not stop with the Old Testament. The demoniac of Gadara was also a cutter.

This man lived in the burial caves and could no longer be restrained, even with a chain. Whenever he was put into chains and shackles—as he often was—he snapped the chains from his wrists and smashed the shackles. No one was strong enough to subdue him. Day and night he wandered among the burial caves and in the hills, howling and cutting himself with sharp stones (Mark 5:3-5).

The act of self-mutilation has become frequent in America. It has a far darker influence then we may be willing to admit. Research tells us that:

- Each year, 1 in 5 females and 1 in 7 males engage in self-injury.
- 90 percent of people who engage in self-harm begin during their teen or pre-adolescent years.
- Nearly 50 percent of those who engage in self-injurious activities have been sexually abused.

- Females comprise 60 percent of those who engage in self-injurious behavior.

- About 50 percent of those who engage in self-mutilation begin around age 14 and carry on into their 20s.

- Many of those who self-injure report learning how to do so from friends or from self-injury websites.

- Approximately two million cases are reported annually in the U.S.[15]

There is no doubt that cutting has an evil influence as mutilation on the outside is a reverse attempt to heal wounds that cannot be touched on the inside. This generation is crying louder, and mutilation is a futile attempt to be heard. Unfortunately they are getting no response from a powerless church that has a lot of noise but no ability to bring freedom.

Many of our American worship events have the best lighting, sound, presentation, musicians, and organization ever. Our churches are well organized and scripted for the best performance. The end result, however, is that there is no reply from heaven because all of it is done in the strength of men and not the power of God. The consequence is that a generation has been left to injure themselves, not only physically, but morally and spiritually as well. Aren't many church gatherings just that too?

The style of Baal worship and our American styles of worship and church services look very much alike. It was loud, there was dancing and movement, and it lasted a long time! How can we know what is real or false? A miraculous life change! A show of the flesh that leaves the worshiper the same, tied to bondages without a word from heaven, does not originate in the heart of God. Isaiah cried out:

> *Oh, that you would burst from the heavens and come down! How the mountains would quake in your presence! As fire causes wood to burn and water to boil,*

15. Samantha Gluck, "Self-Injury, Self-Harm Statistics and Facts," HealthyPlace, August 24, 2012, accessed January 02, 2017, http://www.healthyplace.com/abuse/self-injury/self-injury-self-harm-statistics-and-facts/.

your coming would make the nations tremble. Then your enemies would learn the reason for your fame! When you came down long ago, you did awesome deeds beyond our highest expectations. And oh, how the mountains quaked! For since the world began, no ear has heard and no eye has seen a God like you, who works for those who wait for him! (Isaiah 64:1-4).

This was the heart of Elijah on Mount Carmel—for God to show up from heaven and show the nation and a new generation His power!

In 2001, we planted the church we are presently pastoring. Each year we moved forward with vision, from rented facilities to our present campus. Each year was a new building project, vision campaign, or restructuring for present and future growth. There was staff to hire, vision to cast, people to disciple, problems to manage, and victories to celebrate. It has really been the grace of God to bring us from nine people on a launch team to where we are today, and we are truly grateful to the Lord. One evening in prayer before we began this ministry, I sensed the voice of the Lord, saying, *If anything happens* (referring to what we were starting), *it will not be because of you, but in spite of you.* That wasn't false humility. The reality of church planting has proven that without divine help, we can do nothing.

Recently, I went away to fast and pray just to get a sense of God's voice amidst all the noise that surrounded me. We were in a planning project for future growth again as we needed additional space. It's important in the course of our lives we get alone and get sincerely quiet so we can listen to Jesus. When I returned, I seemed to hear the Lord say something profound, and yet His question to me was simple: *With all the things you are planning, why don't you make Me your next project?* All we were doing was not wrong, but sometimes Jesus gets lost in the mix. He wants to be the center of everything.

> **"With all the things you are planning, why don't you make Me your next project?"**

All the prophets of Baal were lost in their art of worship and God was not responding. I challenge you right now, in the light of a nation that appears angry and confused, a government that has lost its way, and a church that is shouting without an answer, set yourself apart with Christ and desire Him only. Fire will fall from heaven!

It's quite astounding that the prophets of Baal kept asking, even though no one answered. We sometimes think people without a relationship with God aren't praying. Facts suggest differently. Heathens are praying right now. Some pray to alcohol, some to sex, business, or titles and positions. Some pray to Muhammad, Krishna, Joseph Smith, Charles Taze Russell, a cult leader, or other false spiritual leader, looking for answers that aren't going to come.

Do you remember the story of Jonah? As he was on that ship during the terrible storm, those on the boat were praying to their gods to save them. They were hoping someone out there would hear and rescue their lives. That storm did not happen because those on the boat didn't know God but because of a disobedient prophet asleep in the hold of the boat. Is it possible that the chaos in America is not due just to the sins of the nation but the disobedience of a sleeping church who has abdicated its role in its culture as the voice of a living God?

Remember, Israel had turned itself over to Baal worship. The lack of rain on the nation was a result of a group of people who knew better. God sent Elijah to stir the nation back to a relationship with the only God who could save them. God is preparing hearts right now to be the voice to a nation and disobedient church, reminding them that He still rules in the affairs of men. You are coming out of your hiding place and your voice will be filled with the power of God to call the holy fire of judgment and the rain of revival to awaken a nation to the Lord!

Chapter 6
The Fire and the Rain

R evivals do not occur in spiritual vacuums but among people who have prepared their hearts at the prompting of the Lord. In the construction of the tabernacle, God told Moses to *"make everything according to the pattern"* (Exodus 25:40). The pattern was what God had already implemented in heaven, and His desire was to duplicate it here on earth. We cannot create our own design and expect God to fill it. Elijah did six simple things. These were not complicated but were necessary to bring the rain in his day and in ours.

Elijah Repaired the Altar

The constant abuse of the altar by Jezebel's administration had damaged and made it unusable for additional sacrifices. Elijah knew that order preceded glory. Something had to be fixed before it could be used. By God's direction, the purpose of the altar was threefold:

The altar was a place of sacrifice and death.

God established the process of sacrifice in the garden of Eden after Adam and Eve had sinned. The shedding of blood from an innocent animal was the pattern all through Israel's history. Abraham established his relationship with God and the future of the nation as an altar builder. An altar was where sacrifice took place, and for Abraham it was most notably the near sacrifice of his own child, a representation of when God the Father would offer His own Son. The cross became God's final altar when the fire of God's judgment fell on the perfect sacrifice of Jesus. The New Testament makes it clear that we now offer our own bodies as living sacrifices, dead to ourselves yet alive to Christ.

> *And so, dear brothers and sisters, I plead with you to give your bodies to God because of all he has done for you. Let them be a living and holy sacrifice—the kind he will find acceptable. This is truly the way to worship him. Don't copy the behavior and customs of this world, but let God transform you into a new person by changing the way you think. Then you will learn to know God's will for you, which is good and pleasing and perfect* (Romans 12:1-2).

When I offer my life to God, I am to die to myself and live for Christ.

> *My old self has been crucified with Christ. It is no longer I who live, but Christ lives in me. So I live in this earthly body by trusting in the Son of God, who loved me and gave himself for me* (Galatians 2:20).

The altar was the place of consecration.

The psalmist commanded, "*Take the sacrifice and bind it with cords on the altar*" (Psalms 118:27).

God's altar had four horns, or corners, on which sacrifices could be tied securely. This was done to keep the animal from falling off and to hold it in place so the priest could successfully complete his duty. When we offer ourselves to the Lord, we bind ourselves to His purpose, plan, and covenant. We are securely tied so we don't get off the altar and walk away. We offer ourselves to Christ in complete obedience so the Lord can finish His work within us.

The altar was the place of anointing.

When God was giving instructions to Moses regarding the tabernacle, he specifically told Moses to:

Take the anointing oil and anoint the tabernacle and everything in it; consecrate it and all its furnishings, and it will be holy. Then anoint the altar of burnt offering and all its utensils; consecrate the altar, and it will be most holy (Exodus 40:9-10 NIV).

An altar without anointing from God is a powerless altar. The word *anoint* means to smear or rub with oil. My personal time with the Lord determines my public anointing before people and whether or not I have been rubbed with the oil of heaven before people. This might help explain why many churches no longer have altar calls and why seeking God at a public, corporate altar is now discouraged.

If I haven't spent time with Jesus privately, I will not see a need to call a congregation together to seek the Lord. The Spirit of Elijah calls people back to the altar! A church that doesn't have an altar is like a museum that houses things that used to be alive but are now dead. God is calling pastors to reinstitute the altar in their churches. He is calling the entire body of Christ back to personal altars to put the fire of God back in our souls!

Elijah Reconciled the Nation with a Prophetic Act

At this time, Israel was a divided nation. After the death of Solomon, the kingdom split and Rehoboam, Solomon's son, ruled over the southern kingdom of Judah, and Jeroboam led the northern kingdom, often referred to as Israel, Ephraim, or Samaria, which is where Elijah prophesied. There was constant conflict between these two kingdoms. God never intended they be divided but unified. All of the kings of Israel were ungodly, which is why they were taken into captivity before Judah.

They stopped being the powerful nation God intended because of insecure leaders who failed to completely surrender to the will of God. As a result the people became racially, economically, politically, and spiritually divided. Does this not sound familiar today? Civil discussion from real statesmen has been replaced by name calling and divisive rhetoric. This is not evident just in the nation, but in the church as well. I have never understood why individuals who split churches think that the blessing of the Lord will rest on their ministry. Stealing a group of people from one location to another because of an inflated ego is never God's plan. The damage in these kinds of situations are innocent people, especially the next generation who become disillusioned with a real relationship with God and check out of church, so they don't have to worship in an atmosphere of controversy. That's why the words of Psalm 133 are so important:

> *How wonderful and pleasant it is when brothers live together in harmony! For harmony is as precious as the anointing oil that was poured over Aaron's head, that ran down his beard and onto the border of his robe. Harmony is as refreshing as the dew from Mount Hermon that falls on the mountains of Zion. And there the Lord has pronounced his blessing, even life everlasting.*

Unity brings the presence of God and powerful anointing that flows from those leading at the top all the way down the chain of those in charge. Elijah understood this, and even though the nation was divided he took twelve stones, representing the twelve tribes of Israel, and used those stones to rebuild the altar, declaring that one day they would again be united at the altar of the Lord!

I want you to think about the things in your life that seem divided and hopeless. Pause right now and speak a prophetic word over your life, family, relationships, and everything that seems confusing. Make a declaration of healing, peace, provision, and unity in Jesus' name! As you do, you'll prepare the way for fire from heaven to fall!

Elijah Created an Impossible Situation

Read the description of his actions:

Then he dug a trench around the altar large enough to hold about three gallons. He piled wood on the altar, cut the bull into pieces, and laid the pieces on the wood. Then he said, "Fill four large jars with water, and pour the water over the offering and the wood." After they had done this, he said, "Do the same thing again!" And when they were finished, he said, "Now do it a third time!" So they did as he said, and the water ran around the altar and even filled the trench (1 Kings 18:32b-35).

Elijah was creating circumstances in which only the one true God could succeed. Only He could lap up water with fire from heaven. Baal worshipers had ingenious ways to bring fire up from the ground. Elijah made sure that there would be no doubt the fire was from Jehovah. He created an impossible situation that only God could fix. Some of you reading this book are in seemingly impossible circumstances right now. We tend to blame the Devil for this, but God is setting you up for a miracle. Sometimes God will create an impossible situation just to show that He is God as we put our trust in Him. Consider that our nation is now facing impossible odds. God arranges these kinds of circumstances so we will hopefully turn our eyes back on Him. Get ready because nothing is impossible with God!

Elijah Prayed a Short, Simple Prayer

The time of the evening sacrifice was around three in the afternoon. *We can pray short, simple prayers in public when we have prayed long, effectual prayers in private.* One of the reasons our public prayers are anemic is because we spend no private time with God. We will have no more power praying in the name of Jesus publicly than the degree to which that name has possessed us privately. Elijah has spent three and half years spending time with God in preparation for this moment of supernatural encounter. Elijah was not jumping, cutting, or dancing. He was praying. It was a simple prayer that came from a heart of obedience.

The Elijahs of God

O Lord, God of Abraham, Isaac, and Jacob, prove today that you are God in Israel and that I am your servant. Prove that I have done all this at your command. O Lord, answer me! Answer me so these people will know that you, O Lord, are God and that you have brought them back to yourself (1 Kings 18:36-37).

This prayer was not about Elijah but the honor of God. Everything he did on this day was not an idea that came from his own mind, a business meeting, or the latest church conference. The entire confrontation on this mountain came directly from the board room of God. Is it possible to have a good idea without a God idea? Is it possible that we have depended too much on our own creativity instead of spending time with the Lord to listen to His plan?

> **We can pray short, simple prayers in public when we have prayed long, effectual prayers in private.**

Please say the next word with me out loud: "Fire!"

Then the fire of the Lord fell and consumed the burnt offering and the wood and the stones and the dust, and licked up the water that was in the trench. When all the people saw it, they fell on their faces; and they said, "The Lord, He is God; the Lord, He is God" (1 Kings 18:38-39 NASB).

The fire came not from the ground up but from heaven down. Not from the ability of men but the power of God. Fire only falls on sacrifices prepared at the direction of the Lord in obedience to His command. If all of our effort has not produced changed lives that honor God, displayed the supernatural, and caused people to bow down and say *"the Lord, he is God,"* then we have operated in our own religious flesh. Everything on this altar was consumed and burnt up, even the dust. It doesn't matter to God if your wood is wet or dry. Heaven's fire always consumes the dusty relics of our flesh and leaves what God is pleased with.

The Fire and the Rain

The Bible records literal fire falling from heaven numerous times. Several of those instances were judgments, but on at least three of those occasions it was in response to obedient servants. God confirmed His will and lit up heaven to show His pleasure.

David offered a sacrifice of repentance on the threshing floor of Araunah the Jebusite to atone for his sin of numbering the people, and God responded with heavenly fire (1 Chronicles 21:26). Fire consumed the sacrifice at the dedication of Solomon's temple (2 Chronicles 7:1) and here on the top of Mount Carmel. Each time God was placing His stamp of approval as men desired to honor Him. He will cause holy fire to burn in His church again to draw a backslidden nation to Himself.

Elijah Does What Is Possible So God Can Do the Impossible

As soon as the fire fell from heaven, everyone acknowledged that God, not Baal, was to be worshiped. But the fire did not eliminate the prophets of Baal. They would continue to speak, if something wasn't done to silence their voice.

> *Then Elijah commanded, "Seize all the prophets of Baal. Don't let a single one escape!" So the people seized them all, and Elijah took them down to the Kishon Valley and killed them there* (1 Kings 18:40).

As powerful as this event was, it became Elijah's responsibility to make sure all of the prophets of Baal were silenced. God may touch our lives with a mighty move of His Spirit, but it becomes our responsibility to identify the baals in our lives and get rid of them! What is dishonoring to the Lord must go! He will help us, but we must make the choice to let go and let God have His perfect way. Church and governmental leaders need to identify those people in their organizations who don't have the spirit of truth and make preparations to remove them from any additional influence. Pray right now and ask Him to reveal anything displeasing to Him within you. We can do all things through Christ. You can have complete freedom!

The Elijahs of God

Elijah Enforces the Will of God through Intercession

The fire was not the revival. Don't miss that. The fire only prepared the way for the revival. Up to now, there still hadn't been any rain. The ground was still parched, people and animals were still dying of thirst, and lack of moisture had caused fires to break out all across the nation.

Elijah's word to the king was, "*Go get something to eat and drink, for I hear a mighty rainstorm coming!*" (1 Kings 18:41).

> **Hearing in the spiritual realm is a prerequisite for revival as we must lead others into the realty of awakening.**

No one else but Elijah could hear the sound of rain. But spiritual ears can discern what others cannot see or hear. Spending time with the Lord causes us to hear what no one else can hear, see what others cannot see, and do what only those with supernatural faith can do. At first, you will be in the minority, as only a few are sensitive enough to possess sufficient spiritual insight. Hearing in the spiritual realm is a prerequisite for revival as we must lead others into the realty of awakening. Walking into church one evening, the Lord spoke to my heart and said, *Stop looking at those people who don't want Me and start looking at those who do.* We cannot be discouraged when those around us don't understand what we are hearing from the Lord. Soon, God will manifest Himself and all will benefit from those who have spent time with Christ.

Next Elijah climbed to the top of Carmel, the same place that was supposed to be the center of Baal worship, and began to pray for rain. God will always reestablish His authority in places of idolatry. Consider the many places across this nation that at one time, from our nation's founding, were dedicated to the honor of the Lord. Today they are only a shadow of God's original intent. There is a sound in the atmosphere of heaven. The living God is preparing to take back what rightfully belongs to Him. God does the same thing in our lives. He can restore what the enemy has stolen and bring us back into full fellowship with Him.

Elijah gets in the birthing position of a Hebrew woman with his face between his knees to pray because he is getting ready to birth a spiritual awakening for the nation. One might pose this question: Why is it necessary to pray for something God already promised He would do? Didn't the Lord say He was going to send rain?

Throughout the Scriptures, there are many promises of God. But it becomes evident that for those promises to be fulfilled, someone must pray because *prayer enforces the will of God.*

Do you remember the story of Isaac and Rebekah? Isaac had inherited everything his father Abraham had owned including the promises of God for a seed that would be as numerous as the sands on the seashore and would eventually bless the world in Christ. It's obvious the Lord joined Isaac and Rebekah together in Genesis 24 to continue the promises of God given to Abraham. There was only one problem: After they were married it became obvious Rebekah was unable to have children. It appeared that the promise of God would need to stop with her.

When we initially receive a word from the Lord, there is great anticipation for its fulfillment. Sometimes, however, obstacles, circumstances, and the cares of life choke out the promise and we assume it wasn't the will of God at all. At that point we give up. Only eternity will tell how many near revival misses there have been and how many promises have gone unfulfilled because we became weary in well-doing.

The Bible says, *"Isaac pleaded with the Lord on behalf of his wife, because she was unable to have children. The Lord answered Isaac's prayer, and Rebekah became pregnant with twins"* (Genesis 25:21). Isaac would not accept barrenness as a reality because he knew the promise of God. He enforced the will of God through prayer and God answered. This was not a problem for God. Nothing is impossible with Him.

The Elijahs of God

Elijah began this prayer meeting to enforce the will of God for rain on the land. He sent his servant six times to see if there was a response from God. Each time there was nothing. At this point we might get discouraged, but Elijah kept praying. Someone once told me that it would be a lack of faith to pray for something more than once. That's an incorrect teaching that unfortunately has made its way through the Christian world. If that were true, then Jesus prayed in unbelief because on the night before His crucifixion, He prayed the same prayer three different times in the garden (Matthew 26:44)! Jesus also reminds us to:

> *Keep on asking, and you will receive what you ask for. Keep on seeking, and you will find. Keep on knocking, and the door will be opened to you. For everyone who asks, receives. Everyone who seeks, finds. And to everyone who knocks, the door will be opened* (Luke 11:9-10).

Someone might ask, "Isn't this begging God?" No. Baal worship is begging because Baal couldn't make or fulfill promises. Persistent prayer is simply waiting for the Lord to do what He has already promised at the proper time.

One of the clear evidences of an individual or church that is committed to revival is the prayer meeting. I realize corporate prayer and fasting has become a relic, but the biblical and historical precedent to awakening has never been worship music, preaching, or guest relations. It has always been people who gathered together and sought God for His fire to fall in their churches. Someone asked me once why we couldn't just pray at home. We should be praying at home! But a corporate prayer meeting produces corporate results. If you can't find a prayer meeting on your church's calendar, ask the church leadership to start one. If they are unwilling, get out! Nothing but fleshly results can come from an organization that isn't empowered by the Holy Spirit.

You can be sure if church leaders aren't prioritizing public prayer, they sure aren't praying in private. The sacred cows of our glitz and gold must be replaced by men and women whose hearts burn for the living God.

The Fire and the Rain

Quite frankly, if we were raising the dead in our meetings we would not need all those gymnastics to get people to church. The compromise among high-profile religious leaders regarding serious doctrinal and moral issues is further proof they are enemies of the cross of Christ, more interested in spending time in the presence of men instead of the counsel of the Lord.

Prayer enforces the will of God.

There is a marvelous promise in Isaiah 30:18-21 (NIV):

> *Yet the Lord longs to be gracious to you; therefore he will rise up to show you compassion. For the Lord is a God of justice. Blessed are all who wait for him! People of Zion, who live in Jerusalem, you will weep no more. How gracious he will be when you cry for help! As soon as he hears, he will answer you. Although the Lord gives you the bread of adversity and the water of affliction, your teachers will be hidden no more; with your own eyes you will see them. Whether you turn to the right or to the left, your ears will hear a voice behind you, saying, "This is the way; walk in it."*

At the moment when it seemed hope was lost, Elijah sent his servant once more and this time the answer was different: *"I saw a little cloud about the size of a man's hand"* (1 Kings 18:44). You need to have really good eyesight to see a cloud that small.

It wasn't much, but it was all Elijah needed. We must remember not to despise the day of small things. Elijah warned Ahab to take shelter before the rain overwhelmed him. At that moment, the supernatural power of God came on Elijah and he actually outran Ahab's chariot!

> *And soon the sky was black with clouds. A heavy wind brought a terrific rainstorm, and Ahab left quickly for*

The Elijahs of God

> *Jezreel. Then the Lord gave special strength to Elijah. He tucked his cloak into his belt and ran ahead of Ahab's chariot all the way to the entrance of Jezreel* (1 Kings 18:45-46).

Ahab was staying at his winter home in Jezreel about twenty-five miles away. When God broke through with rain, supernatural strength came on Elijah, and he outran Ahab's horse-driven chariot. This is always the goal of revival. There is a visible manifestation to the entire nation of the ability of God to do the impossible and defend His honor. This is why we must move beyond political rhetoric as arguments about conservatism, liberalism, or being on the left or right cannot satisfy the deepest needs of the soul. They only leave people empty. An encounter with Jesus is available when God pours out His Spirit.

In the fall of 2016, the western part of North Carolina was on fire. Multiple outbreaks burned thousands of acres. In addition, the eastern part of the state had been flooded from the rains of Hurricane Matthew. One Sunday morning, a clear prophetic word was given that what we were seeing in the natural was getting ready to happen in the spiritual. We sensed the Lord was saying:

> *"As fire burns up old wood and undergrowth, so I am sending a cleansing fire on My people. What is dead shall be burnt to ashes. That which is unusable shall disappear with the fire and the warmth of My Spirit. What you have struggled with will no longer be a struggle as My fire from heaven will destroy the flesh in your life and cause you to walk in freedom. You will need to fight no longer as My fire will overwhelm every area of weakness. When I am through with the fire, I will then send refreshing rain upon you. As spring brings a fresh cleansing and flowers again appear on the earth, so the floodwaters from My rain will sprout new growth from seeds that have been lying dormant in the deepest parts of your spirit. Life will then come from death as My fire and rain will bring an awakening so powerful that no power of hell shall be*

able to stop it, and you shall know Me in all the fullness of My glory. Prepare yourselves. Fire and rain is at your door."

Things are getting ready to shift. Expect it. The fire and rain are coming!

Chapter 7
Blindsided

Have you ever found yourself in moments when it seemed as if life could not get any better, only to go from that sense of emotional peace to the realization that what you thought was permanent has suddenly changed for the worse? This is what happened to Elijah. It appeared as if nothing would be able to shake him from the experience of fire from heaven and praying through to a mighty rainstorm and finally watching the God of Israel break through and fulfill His word to the nation. But that's where the real test for Elijah began.

Some of our greatest lows come on the heels of some of our greatest highs. You'll remember how Jesus, after being baptized by John and hearing the voice of His Father's approval, was immediately led by the Spirit into the wilderness to be tempted by the Devil (Mark 1).

> **Some of our greatest lows come on the heels of some of our greatest highs.**

The enemy of your soul is not about to let your spiritual victory go unchallenged. Peter reminds us to, *"Stay alert! Watch out for your great enemy, the devil. He prowls around like a roaring lion, looking for someone to devour. Stand firm against him, and be strong in your faith"* (1 Peter 5:8-9).

That's why we must not become overconfident lest we become blindsided by the schemes of hell. At first glance, it would appear that

The Elijahs of God

Elijah simply became fearful because of the words of a female leader in the government who threatened his life. But that is not what happened.

Several years ago, my wife and I were ministering in a very conservative church. I don't just mean conservative theologically but in dress and appearance as well. During the service, a word came forth about the presence of the spirit of Jezebel in the house of the Lord. Of course, they were referring to my wife, who was ministering with me and had makeup on in front of the entire church.

Oftentimes you'll hear someone refer to an individual as a Jezebel because of their outward appearance. That has nothing to do with the real Jezebel. What Elijah was dealing with wasn't a person but a demonic, genderless entity known as the spirit of Jezebel. This spirit is so strong that Elijah could confront 850 false prophets who had challenged his prophetic authority with complete cofidence but ran like a rabbit when this demon made a threat to his life.

In order to understand how significant this is in our culture and how to identify when we are being influenced by Jezebel, the late John Paul Jackson wrote:

> A Jezebel spirit is a celestial power that has worldwide influence. It is not simply a demon that possesses an individual. It is a demonic power in the heavenly realm that transcends specific geographical boundaries and can affect nations. Whatever region this power enters, it cojoins and collaborates with the ruling principality of that territory. Jezebelic powers operate in conjunction with principalities and powers that torment people (Ephesians 6:12). These demonic powers include spirits of religion, manipulation, control, lust, perversion, and the occult. These spirits often work in concert with a Jezebel spirit to build strongholds in a person's mind.[16]

---

16. John Paul Jackson, *Unmasking the Jezebel Spirit* (Carol Stream, IL: Streams House Publishing, 2014), pg 2, 3.

Let's examine some of the characteristics of the Jezebel spirit so we can clearly understand what is happening in America, our government, and our churches and not be led astray by this spiritual being.

The spirit of Jezebel opposes everything righteous, godly, holy, and pure.

> *While Jezebel was killing off the Lord's prophets, Obadiah had taken a hundred prophets and hidden them in two caves, fifty in each, and had supplied them with food and water* (1 Kings 18:4 NIV).

The goal of a Jezebel spirit is to shut down any voice that speaks for the living God. She is the enemy of all that is good. Her desire is to silence the anointing of the Holy Spirit through fear, intimidation, moral or financial failure, and if necessary the death of anyone who threatens her control. This can be attempted through lies, anti-Christian government legislation, pressure to act in a politically correct manner, or through doctrinal error. One of the clear evidences of the Jezebel spirit is the subtle suggestion that faith should be private. Those under its influence say it's okay to keep faith inside the four walls of a church. Anything beyond that is unnecessary and potentially offensive. Be wary of anyone who will not speak publicly of their supposed faith in Christ.

After the healing of a crippled man in Acts 4, the authorities commanded the apostles to stop speaking publicly about Christ.

> *So they called the apostles back in and commanded them never again to speak or teach in the name of Jesus. But Peter and John replied, "Do you think God wants us to obey you rather than him? We cannot stop telling about everything we have seen and heard"* (Acts 4:18-20).

As many miracles continued to occur, they were once again confronted because of their outspoken faith:

> *They brought the apostles before the high council, where the high priest confronted them. "We gave you*

> *strict orders never again to teach in this man's name!"*
> *he said. "Instead, you have filled all Jerusalem with*
> *your teaching about him, and you want to make us*
> *responsible for his death!" But Peter and the apostles*
> *replied, "We must obey God rather than any human*
> *authority"* (Acts 5:27-29).

The parents of Moses were bold enough to trust God with their newborn child:

> *It was by faith that Moses' parents hid him for three*
> *months when he was born. They saw that God had*
> *given them an unusual child, and they were not afraid*
> *to disobey the king's command* (Hebrews 11:23).

> **The time has come for Christians to decide if their faith is going to be public or private. We are approaching the time when civil disobedience in regard to faith will be necessary.**

The time has come for Christians to decide if their faith is going to be public or private. We are approaching the time when civil disobedience in regard to faith will be necessary. The Elijahs of God will not be ashamed to share their faith, no matter the cost. Jesus died openly and naked in front of the entire world! Those who claim only a private faith have no relationship with the Lord and are agreeing with a spirit of Jezebel, speaking her words.

The spirit of Jezebel is fiercely independent.

The Hebrew meaning for *Jezebel* carries the idea of being "un-husbanded,"[17] which refers to a lack of submission to authority. The Scripture speaks about four kinds of authority instituted by the Lord—

---

17. Orr, James, M.A., D.D. General Editor. "Entry for 'JEZEBEL'". "International Standard Bible Encyclopedia". 1915.

civil, governmental, familial, and spiritual. God always operates through His delegated authorities. Even though Jezebel was married and should have understood respect for her husband and her proper role as a queen, Jezebel would submit to no authority in any realm. A Jezebel always bucks those who are in charge. The Septuagint, a Greek translation of the Hebrew Scriptures, adds these words to the threat on Elijah's life:

> *"And Jezabel sent to Eliu, and said, If thou art Eliu and I am Jezabel,"* or "You are Elijah and I am Jezebel" (1 Kings 19:2), implying she was equal with the prophet.[18]

The spirit of Jezebel has no respect for chains of authority and thinks she is equal to those God has appointed. Whenever someone says, "I'll submit to God, but I won't submit to you," they are revealing their true spirit. We can clearly see this happening across our nation right now. The advancement of lawlessness, disrespect to law enforcement, rebellion to parents and church leaders we see in our time is clear evidence that the spirit of Jezebel is at work.

There is a difference between someone who is simply strong-willed or has leadership capabilities and those under the influence of Jezebel. The Jezebel spirit will find ways to take and keep control, no matter who is in charge. Sometimes this is done through outright intimidation; other times it is done through subtle manipulation or a combination of the two through a controlling spirit. They will not take counsel or listen to advice and have no room for someone else's opinion. First Kings 18:19 makes it clear that even though Ahab held the position of king, Jezebel held the power, particularly the ability to financially control those under her influence.

---

18. Janet Howe Gaines, "How Bad Was Jezebel?" *Bible Review* 16.5 (2000): p. 23. According to Sir Lancelot C.L. Brenton's note, the translation of the entire line is, "And Jezabel sent to Eliu, and said, If thou art Eliu and I am Jezabel, God do so to me, and more also, if I do not make thy life by this time tomorrow as the life of one of them."

The Elijahs of God

Now summon all Israel to join me at Mount Carmel,
along with the 450 prophets of Baal and the 400 prophets
of Asherah who are supported by Jezebel.

Jezebel took control of the voices in Israel who were supposed to impartially speak the truth and kept them under her spell by guaranteeing them an income during a famine, thereby feeding them and their families. At the same time, Jezebel allowed the prophets of God to starve. Follow the money. Anyone who is willing to compromise for the sake of an income or wealth has clearly given in to Jezebel. We see this tradeoff of truth all across America right now. From pastors who cuddle up to the top givers in their congregation to politicians who regularly "pay for play" or news media who are more concerned about ratings than truth, Jezebel has inserted herself into every area of our culture.

I have a friend who regularly travels the nation and speaks in many churches in America and around the world. He told me of a church where the pastor pulled out a large white board with the pictures of the top givers. The pastor told my friend if he wanted a big offering to prophesy over those givers. Of course, he wouldn't do it and searched for the "less desirables" in the service that night. This kind of money manipulation goes on in the church and corporate world all the time. We must repent of our desire for the spirit of mammon and ask for the Lord's help to be free from Jezebel if we are to have a nationwide awakening.

The spirit of Jezebel seeks to fill us with fear and makes us want to run from our calling.

When Ahab got home, he told Jezebel everything Elijah
had done, including the way he had killed all the prophets
of Baal. So Jezebel sent this message to Elijah: "May the
gods strike me and even kill me if by this time tomorrow
I have not killed you just as you killed them." Elijah was
afraid and fled for his life (1 Kings 19:1-3).

Does this make any sense? Elijah had just confronted King Ahab and 850 false prophets by himself and was now running for his life! That's because Elijah wasn't dealing with a woman but a demonic spirit. Be aware, especially after a great success, of the sudden desire to "get away from it all" and never come back. There have been many marriages, ministries, businesses, and individuals who unexpectedly, for seemingly no reason at all, exited and never returned. They mistakenly thought this was God's direction or suddenly experienced a mid-life crisis and never recognized that an outside force was attempting to keep them from the end goal God had for them.

About eighteen months after planting the church we presently pastor, a man who attended our church walked into my office and said these words: "You're passive. You don't know how to make decisions and you need someone to keep you in line." Of course, that someone to keep me in line was him and a few others who thought it was their responsibility to take over the leadership roles. This was the beginning of several months of a spiritual tug of war that made us want to run away from the clear word the Lord had given us to come to this specific area in the first place.

Over Christmas, we went away for a few days, and during a time of prayer after our return the Lord spoke very clearly that He had called us to pastor this church. I did not realize at the time that I was dealing with a Jezebel spirit working through the influence of these people. Those individuals eventually moved on and God continued to bless us as we would not submit to the words of a demon. If you have felt like running away from your ministry, marriage, or the occupation the Lord has given you, take some time in the secret place to accurately discern the voice of the Lord. Resist the enemy and he will flee!

The spirit of Jezebel spiritualizes everything.

The story of Naboth's vineyard is extremely insightful when understanding how to deal with Jezebel.

> *Now there was a man named Naboth, from Jezreel, who owned a vineyard in Jezreel beside the palace of King*

The Elijahs of God

Ahab of Samaria. One day Ahab said to Naboth, "Since your vineyard is so convenient to my palace, I would like to buy it to use as a vegetable garden. I will give you a better vineyard in exchange, or if you prefer, I will pay you for it."

But Naboth replied, "The Lord forbid that I should give you the inheritance that was passed down by my ancestors."

So Ahab went home angry and sullen because of Naboth's answer. The king went to bed with his face to the wall and refused to eat!

"What's the matter?" his wife Jezebel asked him. "What's made you so upset that you're not eating?"

"I asked Naboth to sell me his vineyard or trade it, but he refused!" Ahab told her.

"Are you the king of Israel or not?" Jezebel demanded. "Get up and eat something, and don't worry about it. I'll get you Naboth's vineyard!"

So she wrote letters in Ahab's name, sealed them with his seal, and sent them to the elders and other leaders of the town where Naboth lived. In her letters she commanded: "Call the citizens together for a time of fasting, and give Naboth a place of honor. And then seat two scoundrels across from him who will accuse him of cursing God and the king. Then take him out and stone him to death."

So the elders and other town leaders followed the instructions Jezebel had written in the letters. They called for a fast and put Naboth at a prominent place before the people. Then the two scoundrels came and sat down across from him. And they accused Naboth before all the people, saying, "He cursed God and the king."

So he was dragged outside the town and stoned to death. The town leaders then sent word to Jezebel, "Naboth has been stoned to death" (1 Kings 21:1-14).

A vineyard represented not only a financial but a spiritual inheritance. Because Ahab was a carnal king, he could not understand why Naboth would not sell him his vineyard. Naboth was not for sale! Thank God for people who are unwilling to sell out the power of God for convenience, money, or a seeker-friendly message that contains no conviction of sin or call to holiness.

Because the entire political, financial, and religious leadership of Israel was now under Jezebel's spell, she convinced them to organize a spiritual occasion in which Naboth was the guest of honor. The discipline of fasting was invoked and the name of God was used to turn the tables on Naboth and have him executed. It is quite possible that many at this celebration did not even realize they were being manipulated by Jezebel because it was perceived as a spiritual event.

Be wary of people who cloak ulterior motives in spiritual terms: "Our pastor is such a man of God, but he sometimes ignores me." "Sally didn't want me to say anything, but she needs prayer so I'm sure she wouldn't mind me sharing this with you."

Jesus warned of a coming time when those who killed the godly will think they were honoring God or doing Him a service (John 16:2). Judas hid his greedy heart by suggesting the expensive perfume should have been sold and the money given to the poor, even though Judas was the real thief. Watch out for people who are sweet on the outside but have danger lurking within.

Proverbs 26:24-25 says, *"People may cover their hatred with pleasant words, but they're deceiving you. They pretend to be kind, but don't believe them. Their hearts are full of many evils."*

I'm always uncomfortable with those who can't have a general conversation about life without using spiritual terms in an attempt to make themselves sound godlier then they really are. Sometimes the most outwardly spiritual people in a church or business are the most dangerous.

The spirit of Jezebel uses charm, flattery, and seduction.

> *Then Jehu went to Jezreel. When Jezebel heard about it, she put on eye makeup, arranged her hair and looked out of a window. As Jehu entered the gate, she asked, "Have you come in peace, you Zimri, you murderer of your master?"* (2 Kings 9:30-31 NIV)

Jehu, the man ordained by God to finally destroy Jezebel, arrived to confront her legacy of evil. She responded by adjusting her appearance to greet him. It is because of this action that many get the silly notion that to wear makeup creates a Jezebel. The text indicates her style of preparation was indicative of harlotry, which would coincide with her commitment to Baal worship. The real issue here is a woman who was attempting to make a last stand to gain intimacy with a person of influence in order to increase her power and maintain her control. It's quite possible she was trying to seduce Jehu, as she had done with many men throughout her reign.

> This spirit attempts to create unhealthy soul ties through counseling, social media, old relationships, or close friends for the purpose of distorting the anointing of the Holy Spirit and wrecking a godly testimony.

The spirit of Jezebel is attracted to those with spiritual power, and make no mistake about it, many men and women of God have been caught in this spirit's trap of lust and perversion, not realizing the spirit of Jezebel was attempting to destroy their ministries. They only discovered this deception after it was too late. Because sexual immorality is always part of the motive of Jezebel, this spirit attempts to create unhealthy soul ties through counseling, social media, old relationships, or close friends for the purpose of distorting the anointing of the Holy Spirit and wrecking a godly testimony. Jehu, as we will discover later, was not deceived by her charm or compliments and gave instructions to cast her down.

The spirit of Jezebel makes us unfruitful.

> *He looked up at the window and called out, "Who is on my side? Who?" Two or three eunuchs looked down at him* (2 Kings 9:32 NIV).

Prior to Jezebel's demise, Jehu asked an important question: Who is on my side? It's similar to the question Elijah asked on Mount Carmel: How long will you waver between two opinions? Jezebel was in the company of eunuchs. A eunuch is a male who, either by physical defect, choice, or force, is unable to have intercourse to produce children. Jezebel has surrounded herself with those unable to reproduce; this suggests that the spirit of Jezebel makes believers, ministries, and churches unable to birth vision and ultimately new births into the kingdom of God. With 80 percent of churches plateauing or in decline and less than 20 percent of churchgoers in a worship service on any given week, we should be frightened enough to look beyond our church bank accounts and realize we have become spiritually bankrupt in the American church.

One of the key characteristics of a Jezebel spirit has been a lack of instruction and desire for personal evangelism. I'm not talking about outdated methods that no longer work in our culture. I'm speaking about a simple desire to influence people for Christ by our own desire to live a life honorable to God that will be ready to give an answer to the hope within us.

All believers have a Christ-given mandate to share the gospel and make disciples. The screaming need of the lost people around us who have an eternity without Jesus ahead of them should make us painfully aware of the state of our mission. Only a church run by Jezebel would dare suggest we have been successful in our evangelism attempts when most of America is still lost. I'm not suggesting there aren't ministries who are winning people to Christ, but let's be real. If there were as many people getting saved as some ministries claim, the cities of America would have been converted multiple times by now.

Jezebel makes us content with false conversions. This may be our greater problem. Saying a prayer without a lifestyle change is Baal worship. Words must be backed up by a decision to repent. The real evidence of a relationship with Jesus is a desire to please the Lord, pray, and spend time in His Word. By that definition, many American Christians have no relationship with God. Jezebel has convinced them that an hour each week in church is enough! The eunuchs in the Bible were tired of being fruitless and decided it was time to rid themselves of Jezebel. May we American believers become brokenhearted about our cold attitudes toward the lost and cry out again for the fresh fire of Holy Ghost conviction and conversion!

The spirit of Jezebel can persist and endure over many changes in leadership.

Jezebel outlived King Ahab, King Ahaziah, and King Jehoram and continued her evil influence. That's the reason some churches can have a pastoral change but nothing changes. There's always a honeymoon period, but then things go back to normal. People get comfortable with old ways and the initial excitement of fresh vision goes away. The same complaints and problems begin to arise that arose before. The pastor decides to leave or is run off by a few controlling people and the cycle repeats itself. We need to recognize that church issues lasting over long periods of time are due to a spirit that has the goal of keeping that church bound in a box of religion. The only way to fix this is to deal with the real issue of Jezebel.

This is also the reason nations can have elections but nothing changes. There is great hope during each election that the new administration will bring revolution, but things seem to stay the same. When there has been significant change, it tends to move people away from biblical truth. America's leaders are clearly under the control of a Jezebel spirit and have been for many years. Most elected leaders are not even aware how darkness manipulates their decisions through evil people who are tools of hell. The only saving grace of the American political system is the few Elijahs of God in government who hold back the constant press of evil and the godly Christians praying for the nation. This is why the apostle Paul reminded the church:

> *To pray for all people. Ask God to help them; intercede on their behalf, and give thanks for them. Pray this way for kings and all who are in authority so that we can live peaceful and quiet lives marked by godliness and dignity. This is good and pleases God our Savior, who wants everyone to be saved and to understand the truth* (1 Timothy 2:1-4).

We would have far greater blessing on our church and government if we would speak to God about leadership instead of each other and ask the Lord to guide and intervene in their decisions.

The spirit of Jezebel generally operates from behind the scenes to manipulate those who are leaders.

This is the area in which the Jezebel spirit is most often misunderstood. We look for a direct attack from people in leadership or circumstances. However, in dealing with issues the solution becomes elusive and we are unable to place a finger on the source of the problem. That's because of behind-the-scenes manipulation. Jezebel is a master of influencing people through secondary sources. It could appear that Naboth's death was the decision of Ahab until we look behind the curtain and see Jezebel at the helm. The threat to Elijah's life came from Jezebel through a messenger. *Because Jezebel is not directly confrontational, she always needs a host to fulfill her wishes.* Keep in mind that it's not possible to have a Jezebel in operation without an Ahab to support her. If the Ahabs and other minions go away, so does her influence.

We've all seen her character in action from the political world to the local church. Politicians make impossible promises to get votes from an uninformed electorate and threaten their opposition by releasing secret information to influence elections. Instead of going directly to the pastor, someone with a church issue speaks to another leader or their spouse, expecting that person to bring up the problem. Through these manipulations, Jezebel is freed from a direct confrontation. He or she is really a coward, desirous of creating a spirit of division.

They ignore the counsel of Christ on how to deal with offenses and take matters into their own hands. Have you ever heard the phrase, "They are talking?" Who are *they*? In our church, we don't entertain the *theys*. If someone is not willing to be upfront about an issue, we don't give talkers a platform to be the tool of Jezebel. Stop using others to do your dirty work! If you don't have the courage for a face-to-face discussion, then take your evil wares someplace else. This applies not only at church but at work, government, in the home, and with all relationships. Sometimes Jezebel will adversely affect a child or family member in order to influence those who are godly and distract them from their mission. We must continually pray the protection of the Lord over our families to keep Jezebel away. Don't be manipulated by this spirit. God has given you the authority to deal with it victoriously.

The spirit of Jezebel enters through any deep wounds and offenses that have never been placed under the lordship of Jesus.

Jezebel was the daughter of Ethbaal, king of the Sidonians. His Phoenician reign as a priest of Astarte was characterized by idolatry and murder as he came to the throne by assassinating the previous king, Phelles. Ahab formed a political alliance with Ethbaal and to solidify the union married Ethbaal's daughter, Jezebel.[19] Because this was a political decision, it was likely she was pawned off to the highest bidder with no concern for her feelings. As a young lady, Jezebel had been brought up with a murderous father in a wealthy, idolatrous city and had learned all the ways of the Phoenician idols. She was taught that to get what you wanted

19. William Smith, entry for "Ahab," *Smith's Bible Dictionary*, (Grand Rapids, MI: Christian Classics Ethereal Library, 1884). p. 22. Public domain.

required force, sex, money, and manipulation[20] without concern for the well-being of others.

No girl can be placed in this kind of atmosphere without developing deep emotional and spiritual wounds. In order to protect herself from further injury, she vowed to always be the one in charge and never allow a man or anyone else to hurt her again. This opened up her spirit to a demonic influence. Any darkness not overtaken by light becomes darker still.

Some of you reading this, male or female, have been wounded in the early years of your life and developed habits that attempt to control others around you. I'm not suggesting you have a Jezebel spirit. I am saying, however, that those hurts must be submitted to Jesus so you do not continue to hurt others. *Otherwise, an open wound can lead to the influence of Jezebel.*

This kind of demonic warfare was the reason Elijah was caught off guard and temporarily ran for his life. But God's grace is so amazing! While Elijah was in the wilderness, he received a fresh revelation about the future of the nation, his own ministry, and how to deal with Jezebel. As we have been caught in the slime of a nation full of Jezebel's reign, God is preparing His people with a fresh word from heaven including the demise of Jezebel and Ahab. God is preparing a great awakening for America! Get ready!

---

20. Dr. William Smith, "Entry for 'Ethbaal,'" *Smith's Bible Dictionary*, 1901, www. biblestudytools.com, accessed March 21, 2017, http://www.biblestudytools.com/ dictionaries/smiths-bible-dictionary/ethbaal.html.

Chapter 8
Throw Her Down

First church was known for their hard work, love, faith, and constant desire to exceed the limitations of the average and prove excellent in everything they did. Many honestly desired to improve and please the Lord. Staff meetings were creative times of vision, and future growth was always in the discussion. Worship services were engaging, and the preaching was interesting and informative. But something seemed to be lacking. With all their planning and good reputation, it seemed that something kept stalling forward movement.

Church growth consultants gave recommendations and new ideas were implemented. Yet results kept falling short of goals, and no one could understand why. Rumors of disturbing, underlying immorality in the church kept surfacing, and discontent among leaders was increasing. Attendance was beginning to wane along with income. In desperation, the pastor called for a time of prayer and fasting. He was the third to lead the church in ten years, and he had seen this pattern before. A godly man, he genuinely wanted the problems to be solved but had no idea how to fix them.

Some of his best leaders whom he trusted had now become openly confrontational to his leadership and their influence in the congregation had the potential to divide the church and destroy its reputation. As a handful of faithful saints began to pray, it became evident the challenges were more spiritual than they wanted to admit. It would take wise and

The Elijahs of God

Spirit-empowered people to identify and deal with the problems at Thyatira First Church, USA.

It sounds like a hypothetical scenario, but this has been repeated hundreds of times over in American churches. There are many practical matters that churches need to deal with every day from mowing the lawns and taking care of facilities to hiring staff, managing budgets, and casting vision. Even low capacity leaders can do a decent job with good people surrounding them.

However, it is the unseen, the unknowable, the nagging things that one cannot easily identify that Jesus wants in the open. In addressing one of the churches in Asia Minor in Revelation 2, He commended the church at Thyatira for the good they had done, but revealed the church had been invaded by an unrelenting spirit called Jezebel.

> **It is the unseen, the unknowable, the nagging things that one cannot easily identify that Jesus wants in the open.**

> *I know all the things you do. I have seen your love, your faith, your service, and your patient endurance. And I can see your constant improvement in all these things. But I have this complaint against you. You are permitting that woman—that Jezebel who calls herself a prophet— to lead my servants astray. She teaches them to commit sexual sin and to eat food offered to idols. I gave her time to repent, but she does not want to turn away from her immorality* (Revelation 2:19-21).

The Greek word for permitting ("allow, tolerate") is a term that means to "to allow one to do as he wishes, not to restrain, to let alone."[21] It carries with it the idea to ignore an obvious problem

---

21. Thayer and Smith, "Greek Lexicon entry for Eao," The KJV New Testament Greek Lexicon."

and let go on. Thyatira had leaders who recognized the problem of Jezebel but chose to leave her alone, either out of fear or in hope that it would go away on its own. Wisdom with confrontation is always required to deal with Jezebel. Without strong leadership, Jezebel's influence will permeate every area of church and governmental life.

In his bestselling book *Positive Personality Profiles*, Dr. Robert A. Rohm identifies the four different personality traits in the DISC Model of Human Behavior. One of those types referred to is the "supportive type," which is a nice person, easy to get along with, and who doesn't like conflict. The majority of people in the general population are in this "supportive type" category.[22] This is significant as most church leaders would identify as non-confrontational, which explains why they are reluctant to have conflict with a Jezebel.

However, regardless of which characteristic someone identifies with, everyone needs to get past leaving Jezebel to herself. This spirit thrives in a non-confrontational atmosphere. It is also significant that Jezebel identified herself as a prophetess. This was a title she gave herself; it was not awarded her by the Lord. Once again, she assumed a position of authority outside the realm of genuine anointing.

In the late 1980s, I was ministering in a series of meetings in northern Maine. I had been asking the Lord why, in the history of this church, had there never been a regional wide spiritual awakening. Even though good things had occurred over the years, the church was now in decline and needed a fresh move of the Spirit. The tendency had been to blame the Devil for the lack of revival. As I knelt to pray one afternoon, the Spirit dropped this Scripture in my heart:

> *I kept the rain from falling when your crops needed it the most. I sent rain on one town but withheld it from another. Rain fell on one field, while another field withered away* (Amos 4:7).

---

22. Robert Rohm, *Positive Personality Insights* (Atlanta, GA: Personality Insights Publishing, 1992).

The Elijahs of God

Suddenly, the Lord opened up to me the reason why revival tarried in this community; it wasn't a result of the Devil's activity but God's hand. Persistent sin, hidden sexual immorality, and a passive approach to issues resulted in God withholding the rain of His Spirit. As I preached this revelation on a Friday evening, the Holy Spirit moved across the congregation and confirmed His word. There was a lady present that night who called herself a prophetess. I briefly spoke with her following the service and then returned to where I was staying.

The following Sunday, she began to prophesy to the church and completely contradicted the word given earlier. She began her "prophetic" word by saying, "It is not Me but it is the Devil," suggesting that God was not responsible for the lack of awakening and ultimately taking all responsibility for sin off the church. I was amazed as I listened to her bring forth this false prophecy and even more amazed when the church leadership said nothing about it. In that moment, she revealed what spirit she was operating in as Jezebel will always contradict a true word from the Lord. To date, that church is in worse condition than ever with only a handful of people left to keep the doors open.

It may seem difficult to deal with Jezebel, but the consequences of non-action are far worse. Sexual immorality and idolatry was increasing in Thyatira and Jesus commanded the church to stop ignoring the root issue. The Lord gave opportunity for repentance as God's heart is to always lead us back to Him. It is not surprising that in Revelation this Jezebel refused to repent and the Lord commanded a swift action of judgment on her and anyone who followed her teaching.

Throw Her Down

When Jehu met Jezebel for the last time, his direction to the eunuchs surrounding her was to, "Throw her down!"

> *Jehu looked up and saw her at the window and shouted, "Who is on my side?" And two or three eunuchs looked out at him. "Throw her down!" Jehu yelled. So they threw*

110

her out the window, and her blood spattered against the wall and on the horses. And Jehu trampled her body under his horses' hooves (2 Kings 9:32-33).

The apostle Paul uses similar language when giving us spiritual warfare instructions:

*For the weapons of our warfare are not carnal but mighty in God for **pulling down** strongholds, **casting down** arguments and every high thing that exalts itself against the knowledge of God, bringing every thought into captivity to the obedience of Christ, and being ready to punish all disobedience when your obedience is fulfilled* (2 Corinthians 10:4-6 NKJV).

The spiritual weapons of holy living, prayer, fasting, wisdom, and faith are given to us so that Jezebel can be thrown down and defeated by believers who are willing to walk in the authority given to us by the Commander of heaven's armies.

> The spiritual weapons of holy living, prayer, fasting, wisdom, and faith are given to us so that Jezebel can be thrown down and defeated by believers who are willing to walk in the authority given to us by the Commander of heaven's armies.

There are some basic principles to remember when dealing with Jezebel:

Remember that your authority comes from the Lord. There need not be any fear as the position you hold has been given to you by Christ to operate on His behalf for the sake of His Kingdom. *"He disarmed the spiritual rulers and authorities. He shamed them publicly by his victory over them on the cross"* (Colossians 2:15).

The Elijahs of God

You must check your own life for any unconfessed sin, unforgiveness, or secret rebellion. To have spiritual authority requires us to be under the authority and lordship of Jesus and in submission to those the Lord has placed over us.

Prepare yourself mentally, physically, and spiritually. This is not a confrontation you can take lightly. Meeting Jesus in the secret place must become your favorite time alone.

Don't go alone. The spirit of Jezebel is famous for becoming the victim and accusing the accusers. You must have witnesses to verify you have operated in the spirit of Christ and have verifiable and documented reasons for your invasion into her world.

Expect the victory and don't run when threatened. The Lord will be your front and rearguard as you obey His direction.

Trust in the promises of God. There is a promise of worldwide spiritual authority to those willing to deal with Jezebel:

> *To all who are victorious, who obey me to the very end, to them I will give authority over all the nations. They will rule the nations with an iron rod and smash them like clay pots. They will have the same authority I received from my Father, and I will also give them the morning star!* (Revelation 2:26-28)

Part 3:

The Elijahs of God Will Call Forth the Next Generation To Righteous Destiny

Chapter 9
Go Back the Way You Came

The news media was in shock. They had never heard or seen such a thing. For years, they had been able to control the narrative of the nation with little opposition. Now reports were coming in from the field that a huge disaster had just occurred and the deaths of hundreds of loyal supporters were being broadcast. Was it an earthquake? A storm? An unprecedented accident that had caused such destruction? Nope. Weathermen were now saying that after three and a half years of drought, it was raining! What was happening? As the investigations began, it was hard to believe that one man was responsible for all the mayhem. His name was Elijah, and now he had disappeared and wasn't speaking to the news media!

> We really don't understand the power of one person completely committed to the will of God.

We really don't understand the power of one person completely committed to the will of God. We often feel the task is too big, the obstacles too large, and the opposition too great for us to make a real difference. We become focused on our limited resources, our lack of personal charisma, our history riddled with failures, and come to the mistaken conclusion that God could surely use someone else to more effectively accomplish His will. Nothing could be further from the truth. The Elijahs of God are not the most popular, talented, wealthy, or well-known people. They make mistakes, get discouraged, and are consciously and painfully aware of their limitations.

The Elijahs of God

The apostle Paul reminds us:

Remember, dear brothers and sisters, that few of you were wise in the world's eyes or powerful or wealthy when God called you. Instead, God chose things the world considers foolish in order to shame those who think they are wise. And he chose things that are powerless to shame those who are powerful. God chose things despised by the world, things counted as nothing at all, and used them to bring to nothing what the world considers important. As a result, no one can ever boast in the presence of God (1 Corinthians 1:26-29).

The Elijahs of God do, however, have one thing in common—an understanding of the greatness of God, the fear of the Lord, and discernment for the hour of crisis to which they have been prepared to engage. They know His honor is at stake, and despite the unknowns they desire to make His name known. With the help of the Lord you can do this, no matter what challenges you are presently facing.

We know the spiritual reasons why Elijah ran from Jezebel. Can you honestly blame him? He was being confronted by one of the most powerful demonic forces ever to be released from hell. He had not expected how it would affect his spirit. But were there other, personal issues that made this attack so devastating? Was something taking place with Elijah that even he wasn't willing to acknowledge?

Through the events that had occurred, we know he had to have experienced extreme anticipation, excitement, and probably some pretty strong emotions when he confronted the 850 false prophets. Add to that the intense physical activity required to rebuild the altar, sacrifice an animal, and then intercede for his nation. Even though the Spirit of the Lord empowered Elijah, the events were taking their toll on his body and mind. It is dangerous for us to think that because we have been anointed by God and have seen miracles occur we can ignore our physical needs. Many a man or woman of God has shifted from anointing to adrenalin without

116

being able to discern the difference and can't understand why the body can't keep up with the move of God.

We learn how significant this was after he fled from Jezebel. He took his servant with him to Beersheba, a distance of about 100 miles. Keep in mind that there is no record that during this time he had anything to eat or drink, and we know he had little, if any, sleep.

What did Elijah do next after this personal challenge was concluded? He disconnected. We disconnect from people too. He stayed with his servant for the first part of his journey then left to be by himself and continue his trip to Mount Sinai, another 200-plus miles.

Three things become evident about Elijah's emotional state at this moment:

He is focused on himself and depressed.

> *Then he went on alone into the wilderness, traveling all day. He sat down under a solitary broom tree and prayed that he might die. "I have had enough, Lord," he said. "Take my life, for I am no better than my ancestors who have already died"* (1 Kings 19:4).

This was Elijah's way to say, "I've had it! I can't take it anymore!" He's asking God to take his life so Elijah would not have to be responsible for his own death. All of this happens in a solitary place without friends or family to encourage him and help straighten out his thinking. When we become self-absorbed, we forget the great things the Lord has done for us. Evidently, what God had just accomplished through him was already a distant memory. It's possible that all of Elijah's personal expectations had not been met as revealed in his statement that he wasn't any better than the generation before him. How important is it that we keep people in our lives and don't allow ourselves to check out for long periods of time? The Bible answers that question:

117

The Elijahs of God

Two people are better off than one, for they can help each other succeed. If one person falls, the other can reach out and help. But someone who falls alone is in real trouble. Likewise, two people lying close together can keep each other warm. But how can one be warm alone? A person standing alone can be attacked and defeated, but two can stand back-to-back and conquer. Three are even better, for a triple-braided cord is not easily broken (Ecclesiastes 4:9-12).

> **The New Testament church would never have survived its cultural pressures had they been taught to be lone rangers.**

When we find ourselves in a low place—either out of embarrassment, offence, fear, failure, or even our own anger with God—we can disconnect from people and develop a distorted view of reality. As a pastor, I've watched many people who were connected at a church drift away during times of crisis. Those who survive difficult times stay close and transparent. God has developed His people for community. The New Testament church would never have survived its cultural pressures had they been taught to be lone rangers. Teachings that tell us that church family or church attendance is not important and corporate worship is not necessary fail to understand why God wants us encouraging one another. There are dozens of verses in the Bible that speak about our interaction with one another. It's really difficult to be with "one another" when we are by ourselves! That's why the Scriptures admonish us to continue meeting together even more as we see the time of Jesus' return approaching (Hebrews 10:25).

Elijah is tired, hungry and worn out.

Then he lay down and slept under the broom tree. But as he was sleeping, an angel touched him and told him, "Get up and eat!" He looked around and there beside his head was some bread baked on hot stones and a jar of water! So he ate and drank and lay down again. Then the angel of the Lord came again and touched him and said, "Get up and eat some more, or the journey ahead will be too much for you." So he got up and ate and drank, and the food gave him enough strength to travel forty days and forty nights to Mount Sinai, the mountain of God (1 Kings 19:5-8).

Elijah had been expending so much energy that when he finally stopped, he dropped! Some people feel they are invincible, but even the most energetic only have so much emotional, spiritual, and physical strength in their reserves. Without replenishing the well, we will eventually run out. All of us need a balance of food and rest. One day while I was in university, a student seemed to literally lose his mind. He seemed uncontrollable in his actions, and no one could console him. One of the professors discovered it had been a lengthy time since the boy had eaten or had any sleep. Instead of trying to cast the Devil out of him, he was given food and put to bed. Problem solved! He just needed food and rest! Sometimes the most spiritual things we can do are practical.

Even Jesus understood this. After being empowered by Christ to do miracles, the disciples came back and reported to Jesus:

The apostles returned to Jesus from their ministry tour and told him all they had done and taught. Then Jesus said, "Let's go off by ourselves to a quiet place and rest awhile." He said this because there were so many people coming and going that Jesus and his apostles didn't even have time to eat. So they left by boat for a quiet place, where they could be alone (Mark 6:30-32).

The natural inclination was to keep ministering, but Jesus knew even the most successful people needed rest. As it was, their rest was interrupted because people kept looking for them. Remember, there will always be needs. That's not a harsh, uncaring statement but a reality of life. God

The Elijahs of God

wants us to have longevity, not burn out at an early age because we did not take care of our bodies. God was teaching Elijah the importance of being able to manage the highs and lows of relationship with God and move through the seasons of his life with the understanding that there will always be another season.

This truth becomes especially important for those with younger children. There are many kids whose parents are so driven to succeed that little time is spent with the children during the most formative years. Many pastors' kids walk away from the Lord during their young adult years because Mom and Dad were more interested in pastoring everyone else instead of their own family.

A while back, it became evident to me that I was running on empty. I realized we are only given so much emotional, physical, and spiritual resources in the course of each day. Work, family, money, and life was draining my strength. I discovered I could choose to spend all of my energies in the first few hours of the day or learn to pace myself so I would have something left to give when I arrived home in the evening. It meant that I would need to discern those issues and decisions I involved myself in and those that did not really need my input. To do this, I needed the wisdom and discernment of God. Our continual connection to Him cannot be understated.

Long distance or endurance runners also understand they cannot use all their energies in the first few moments of a race. Otherwise they won't be able to cross the finish line. Additionally, too many runs in a short amount of time depletes their energy. Men and woman who don't take care of themselves, are overweight, and never take time off may look spiritual but are only fooling themselves. They may have great minds, but without the physical stamina to endure they will fall short of God's best. One of the most spiritual things some people can do is take a vacation and not feel guilty about it or let others make them feel guilty. The Elijahs of God learn that the Lord is more interested in the minister than the ministry and will not allow others to set their calendar. It's evident that even though Elijah was worn out, he still had a divine connection. An angel prepared a meal and woke him up twice to eat. The supernatural grace of God is available no matter what situation we find ourselves in; only supernatural help can sustain us.

Elijah had lost his sense of reality.

God asked him what he was doing. God often asks questions in order to help us see the answer. Elijah's response revealed that his vision had become myopic and all about himself.

> *He replied again, "I have zealously served the Lord God Almighty. But the people of Israel have broken their covenant with you, torn down your altars, and killed every one of your prophets. I am the only one left, and now they are trying to kill me, too"* (1 Kings 19:14).

Many of us find ourselves in circumstances in our lives that are no fault of God's. We are unable to answer simple questions that can give us future direction because we have forgotten that the mission is not about us but God's purpose in us. Elijah has now believed the misinformation that he is the only one left who is still serving the Lord. When we get like this, we think no one else has ever been through the same thing we have endured. Shout to yourself right now, "I'm not the only one!" You're not the only one who has struggled, who has unanswered questions, who feels all alone.

> *The temptations in your life are no different from what others experience. And God is faithful. He will not allow the temptation to be more than you can stand. When you are tempted, he will show you a way out so that you can endure* (1 Corinthians 10:13).

Remember, keeping to yourself like Elijah did will make you feel alone when that's not really true. Elijah's zeal for God had turned inward. Now he was zealous for himself and his own feelings. He forgot about the prophets of Baal who had been killed; he could only remember the bad and not the good that had been done. God did not lecture Elijah but gave

The Elijahs of God

him grace. God was kind to Elijah as He is to us. Through this experience, Elijah learned one of the most important lessons ever in his walk with God.

Elijah learned that God speaks in different ways.

> *"Go out and stand before me on the mountain," the Lord told him. And as Elijah stood there, the Lord passed by, and a mighty windstorm hit the mountain. It was such a terrible blast that the rocks were torn loose, but the Lord was not in the wind. After the wind there was an earthquake, but the Lord was not in the earthquake. And after the earthquake there was a fire, but the Lord was not in the fire. And after the fire there was the sound of a gentle whisper. When Elijah heard it, he wrapped his face in his cloak and went out and stood at the entrance of the cave* (1 Kings 19:11-13a).

A windstorm, an earthquake, and a fire. Those are all dramatic occurrences that God initiated as He passed by Elijah to speak a fresh word to the prophet. Elijah certainly knew about significant, supernatural manifestations, especially fire. Less than two months before, God had spoken with fire from heaven and defeated Baal worship in Israel. Yet this time, none of these divine acts contained the voice of the Lord. It is important to realize that outward signs may not be an indicator that God is speaking. There are many who look only for the visible and think they have heard from God when nothing has been said. Elijah was sensitive enough to not be awed at the outward. God would show him that no matter what he had seen in the past, God always had fresh ways to speak. The same is true for us.

One of the greatest hindrances to the next move of God is the last move of God and what we experienced. We tend to lean to the familiar because it's comfortable. We remember how God showed up in the past and assume that's how it will occur in the future. I've spoken with people who are entirely caught up in a desire for the "old days."

Ecclesiastes 7:10 reminds us, *"Don't long for 'the good old days.' This is not wise."*

> **One of the greatest hindrances to the next move of God is the last move of God and what we experienced.**

When Jesus was born, most were looking for a messiah to come in a different way and missed what God intended for humanity. Paul lets us know, *"the rulers of this world have not understood it; if they had, they would not have crucified our glorious Lord"* (1 Corinthians 2:8).

If we look for awakening based on what we already have experienced, we could miss the next move of God. To hear what we've never heard, see what we've never seen, and do what we've never done will require a new paradigm of faith and trust in the Lord. Paul also wrote:

> *"No eye has seen, no ear has heard, and no mind has imagined what God has prepared for those who love him." But it was to us that God revealed these things by his Spirit. For his Spirit searches out everything and shows us God's deep secrets* (1 Corinthians 2:9-10).

God wants to reveal Himself to us. The Elijahs of God are always open to new, gentle nudges and revelation of the Spirit.

What becomes obvious about God is that He is not angry with Elijah. God shows him the many ways He desires to communicate with His people. Even during the lowest, most discouraging times of our lives, the presence of God is there.

David reminds us in Psalms 139:1-12:

> *O Lord, you have examined my heart and know everything about me. You know when I sit down or stand*

up. You know my thoughts even when I'm far away. You see me when I travel and when I rest at home. You know everything I do.

You know what I am going to say even before I say it, Lord. You go before me and follow me. You place your hand of blessing on my head. Such knowledge is too wonderful for me, too great for me to understand!

I can never escape from your Spirit! I can never get away from your presence! If I go up to heaven, you are there; if I go down to the grave, you are there. If I ride the wings of the morning, if I dwell by the farthest oceans, ***even there your hand will guide me, and your strength will support me.***

I could ask the darkness to hide me and the light around me to become night—but even in darkness I cannot hide from you. To you the night shines as bright as day. Darkness and light are the same to you.

Hallelujah! God is with us even when we feel alone in the wilderness! We may criticize Elijah for running and ending up in a desolate location, but notice what happened next—he went back to the secret place! His natural bent was to return to the spot where intimacy with God could restore his soul. No matter what you are struggling with right now, get back to the secret place and you will hear the voice of God again!

When Elijah responded to the whisper of God, the Lord asked him a second time what he was doing there. When God has to ask us more than once, it probably means we didn't get it the first time around! Aren't you grateful He is patient with us? Elijah responded the same way, only this time he received specific direction about government and spiritual leaders in Israel and how he was to be part of the future of those nations.

The first words from God are significant: "*Go back the way you came.*" Sometimes we must retrace our steps to restart our mission. God wasn't calling Elijah to do something different, just continue with his original call. To do that required a U-turn. If you have gotten off track, stop and do a U-turn. Don't keep moving in the wrong direction. Elijah humbled himself and walked back over territory he didn't think he needed to cover again.

Sometimes, finding the mind of God is not as easy as some would like us to believe. Even with a willing heart, some steps are made in the darkness of faith with only blind trust to lead us.

For several years, we traveled as evangelists, ministering in churches here and abroad. We were also part of a national ministry called Reality Outreach that produced an original, extremely effective, soul-winning drama called "Heaven's Gates and Hell's Flames." We saw thousands of people make commitments to Christ and were part of many significant outpourings of the Holy Spirit. Rudy and Karen Krulik and Al and Maureen Grubb, the founders of this ministry, were amazing people who taught us about the importance of prayer and the secret place.

After several years of traveling, we sensed a call to pastor and began to pursue what we believed was God's desire for us at that time. A local church pastor of an area we were interested in told us he was leaving and wanted us to take his place. We assumed this was God and began making plans to leave the road for the transition. During the process, this pastor changed his mind about leaving. That wasn't a problem except that we still felt called to that area. Unfortunately, that local ministry felt threatened and this began a year of confusion, challenge, broken relationships, and misinformation about our motives.

Because we had now resigned our position with Reality Outreach and in order to support our family, I began scheduling meetings again and flying to preach in various locations in the US. Even though evangelists frequently leave their families for ministry, this was not our original plan. We even considered dropping all ministry credentials and planting a church in the area we thought God was calling us to reach, regardless of the opinions of other people, as our only desire was to obey the Lord.

125

The Elijahs of God

While driving home one day and praying about our situation, I felt the imprint of the hand of God on my chest and heard this word in my spirit—*wait.* That one word made everything clear as it became obvious we were not to move forward with a church plant at that time.

A few months later, an opportunity for church planting was offered to us in Charlotte, North Carolina. We drove to North Carolina and the first night we were there I had a dream. An older prophetic man of God who has since passed away named A.E. Shuttlesworth spoke to me in the dream and told me I was looking in the wrong city! It's not possible for me to put in writing the emotions we were feeling at the time. It was as though no matter how hard we tried, we could not find the mind of God.

After a period of time, Reality Outreach called us and asked if we would consider traveling with their ministry again. At that point we "went back the way we had come before." None of our path made sense but we obeyed the Lord. One evening in my discouragement, I went out to pray, confused as to why I was covering old ground again and seemingly not moving forward.

The Lord said four simple words to me that settled my heart: *"I am with you."* No matter where life takes you, all that matters is that the presence of God is with you.

It would be another two years before the timing of the Lord would be made clear to plant the church we are now pastoring. This came about from a simple prayer and a dream. One evening, I remember telling the Lord, "I'm not smart enough to figure this out on my own. You are going to have to show us exactly where You want us to be." I had not told my wife about the specifics of my prayer. She didn't mention it for a couple of days, but that evening she had a dream. In it, we were at a ministers' gathering, and I came running up to her saying that Charles Kelly, who was the district pastor, felt like we should be in a place outside of Hickory, North Carolina. We had seldom been through this area and this location was not part of our earlier consideration as we were looking at Atlanta, Georgia. Over the next few months, we began to pray about this dream to see if it was from the Lord. It became obvious this was a clear word from heaven, and over the next several months God brought his plan together. Even though the entire process took about three years, we are grateful for the perfect timing of the Lord.

Looking back, we would not change anything as the lessons taught about the voice of God will be with us the rest of our lives. We were not wasting time as we were learning how to discern the different ways the Lord can speak.

If Elijah had sensed a loss of purpose, God quickly reestablished his vision. He was told to designate two kings who would complete the purge of Baal worship that Elijah had begun. Hazael would take control of the Arameans in Damascus, and Jehu would rule over Israel. It would be Jehu who would have Jezebel thrown to the ground and finally destroy her evil influence. As there is no success without a successor, Elisha would continue the powerful ministry of Elijah. To encourage Elijah, the Lord reminded him he was not the only one serving Yahweh. There were still 7,000 who had refused to kiss or bow before the idol of Baal. In spite of what we may see around us, there are still many faithful followers of Christ. Be encouraged—you're not alone!

The Elijahs of God understand their influence can change the direction of nations. Remember, your influence is not just to be local but regional and worldwide as well. I speak over your life right now that you will see your voice extend to the nations of the world and the spirit of Elijah will flow through you like an unhindered river! Arise, Elijahs of God!

Chapter 10
Pass the Mantle

Even though I had wonderful, loving parents, I was not raised in a Christian home. My grandmother, Jean Sewell, affectionately known as "Sister Sewell," was the spiritual influence who would lead me to a relationship with Jesus. Her prayers and the willingness of my sister to take me to church changed my destiny forever. I remember one day as a little boy, sitting in church and listening to an old song that said, *"Come into my heart, come into my heart, come into my heart, Lord Jesus. Come in today, come in to stay, come into my heart Lord Jesus."*[23]

Suddenly, without warning, the Holy Spirit asked me a question. *Do you want what you're singing about?* I said, "Yes!" I remember pushing people aside and walking down the center aisle of that little church and kneeling down at an altar to give my life to Christ. From that moment, everything changed and nothing about my future would ever be the same.

Growing up in that church, there would be frequent moves of the Holy Spirit across the congregation. I'm not talking about man-manipulated worship services, but holy moments when the presence of Jesus was so strong, He could hardly be resisted. God began to show me there was more to serving the Lord than sermons and songs. He taught me that it was necessary to be sensitive to the flow of His Spirit as it was better to have

---

23. "Into My Heart" by Harry D. Clarke © 1924, Ren. 1952 Hope Publishing Company, Carol Stream, IL 60188 www.hopepublishing.com. All rights reserved. Used by permission.

The Elijahs of God

His mind then our own. I learned that the anointing of the Spirit made all the difference in bringing people to freedom in Jesus.

Our youth camps were more than times of entertainment. We went for one reason—to encounter the presence of God. I remember one specific evening when the power of the Lord was poured out on the campground. The teenagers were overwhelmed, and when it came time to close the service, it could not be stopped. The students spread out across the ballfield, falling under the power of God. The camp director got in his truck, picked kids up who were lying on the ground and in the bushes, and got them back to their rooms. One of those years I was overseeing a group of students in a dorm room. As I began the evening devotion before lights out, the Holy Spirit fell again, and for hours into the night Jesus ministered to those in need of freedom. Oh, for the touch of God again on this generation!

After church one evening, we heard a yell from the tabernacle telling us to come quick because Pauline had been healed. Pauline was a young lady in the latter stages of multiple sclerosis. She had been attending that week. She had difficulty walking across the grounds on her crutches as the MS was progressing. As I entered the building, she was at the altar, literally dancing in the Spirit, completely healed! At the end of service that night, she had told the Lord she wasn't leaving until He healed her. Suddenly Pauline saw Jesus at the front, holding His hand out to her, telling her to come to Him. She began to painfully move to the front, crying out, "Jesus, Jesus!" She said it was difficult to get there but as she got closer to Christ, He reached out and their hands touched. Instantly, the power of God moved though her body. The pain left, the muscles began to work, and she was totally and instantaneously healed by the power of God!

I've watched kids in foreign nations, at youth camps where I was ministering, spend hours in church seeking the Lord. Some of these places had multiple services a day, and with my American model in mind, I thought, "This isn't going to work."

Yet each time I preached, it was like a first service. Students flooded the altars, hungry for the Lord. Some of them fasted and prayed all night, asking God to create an atmosphere in which lives would be transformed. Spirit-filled atmospheres are places in which men and woman of God are made, called, and sent out to prophesy to a nation.

David prayed for the next generation to know the Lord;

> *O my people, listen to my instructions. Open your ears to what I am saying, for I will speak to you in a parable. I will teach you hidden lessons from our past—stories we have heard and known, stories our ancestors handed down to us. We will not hide these truths from our children; we will tell the next generation about the glorious deeds of the Lord, about his power and his mighty wonders. For he issued his laws to Jacob; he gave his instructions to Israel. He commanded our ancestors to teach them to their children, so the next generation might know them— even the children not yet born—and they in turn will teach their own children. So each generation should set its hope anew on God, not forgetting his glorious miracles and obeying his commands. Then they will not be like their ancestors—stubborn, rebellious, and unfaithful, refusing to give their hearts to God* (Psalms 78:1-8).

At first glance, we could take a look around our churches on Sunday mornings and say we are doing okay. Our kids are in church most weeks, some of them serve and others come to a youth meeting on a semi-regular basis. Some can even quote Scripture and relate ancient stories from the Bible. This façade, however, may not tell the whole story. If we just base our observations on church kids, we will not get an accurate view of where the next generation is headed.

Research about unchurched millennials, those born between 1984 and 2002, indicates an erosion of belief in God and the Bible. According to the Barna Research Group, only a combined 27 percent believe the Bible is inspired or the actual Word of God. "When asked to identify words they associate with the Bible, non-Christian Millennials are most likely

The Elijahs of God

to place the Bible within cultural mythology than to describe it in terms of the sacred or divine. Their top five word choices are 'story' (50%), 'mythology' (38%), 'symbolic' (36%), 'fairy tale' (30%) and 'historical' (30%). Very few choose words that reflect divine origins: Just 12% of non-Christian Millennials picked the word 'sacred' to describe the Bible, one in 10 chose 'fact' and even fewer selected 'revelation' (8%), 'infallible' (3%) or 'inerrant' (2%)."[24]

It's good that 96 percent of church millennials believe the Bible to be the inspired Word of God except that church kids are in the minority.[25] The fact is that this present generation views the church as boring, judgmental, and hopelessly irrelevant to their lives. In spite of some successful mega churches who are genuinely reaching cites and seeing conversions, much of our perceived growth has been transferred from other church people who are looking for the latest, fashionable ministry on the block. We have been subtly moved from a foundation found only in Christ and assimilated into a self-satisfying, feel-good, consumer-driven, politically motivated, syncretistic religious system that the next generation wants nothing to do with and that we can no longer ignore.

In spite of what we see, though, the news is never bad for God. The history of spiritual awakenings has always moved in cycles from spiritual lows to spiritual highs. From the book of Acts to the Welsh Revival, the First and Second Great Awakenings, and moves of God since man was created, God's desire has always been to invade our culture and personal lives with a fresh understanding of who He is and what He can do. I've been told the day of the move of God is over. I say it is just beginning! *"But as people sinned more and more, God's wonderful grace became more abundant"* (Romans 5:20).

As awakenings move in cycles, so do nations, churches, and individuals. Nations are born in freedom. People fight for, and are willing to die for,

---

24. "Millennials and the Bible: 3 Surprising Insights," Barna Research Group, October 21, 2014, accessed January 02, 2017, https://www.barna.org/barna-update/millennials/687-millennials-and-the-bible-3-surprising-insights#.VcOYyHnbLIU.
25. Ibid.

this freedom. Then the ideals of freedom are forgotten. Leaders begin to compromise, drift away from God, and over time commit apostasy. The founding principles are neglected, and bondage begins to grip the nation. Government becomes oppressive, financial and religious liberties are restricted, morality is compromised, and we become a shadow of our former selves. Most churches begin in the fervor of excitement, pursuing the will of God to bring people to Jesus. Over time, though, we can lose our fire and move from ministry to maintenance and forget the reason for our existence. Enter the Elijahs of God and their anointing on the next generation!

The clear command to Elijah was to find a specific person he could mentor to take his place. That person was Elisha.

> *So Elijah went and found Elisha son of Shaphat plowing a field. There were twelve teams of oxen in the field, and Elisha was plowing with the twelfth team. Elijah went over to him and threw his cloak across his shoulders and then walked away. Elisha left the oxen standing there, ran after Elijah, and said to him, "First let me go and kiss my father and mother good-bye, and then I will go with you!"*
>
> *Elijah replied, "Go on back, but think about what I have done to you." So Elisha returned to his oxen and slaughtered them. He used the wood from the plow to build a fire to roast their flesh. He passed around the meat to the townspeople, and they all ate. Then he went with Elijah as his assistant* (1 Kings 19:19-21).

The Lord spoke to me in prayer one day and said I needed to make a greater investment in the next generation than ever before. God became very specific to Elijah as it was so important to Him that the next generation had a place of influence. God is clearly speaking to us to lay aside our personal preferences and engage the new millennials with the call of God. The Elijahs of God understand that life is not just about their blessing but

The Elijahs of God

passing the mantle of awakening. I often tell people that by the time we turn forty and look over our shoulders, we will see a group of kids following. At that moment, we cannot be thinking about our legacy or biases but about their future.

> **The Lord will pass over someone who spends time in front of an entertainment screen to look for someone who shows initiative and is not lazy.**

It is interesting that Elisha is plowing a field when Elijah finds him. God usually looks for people who already have their hands on some sort of work, whether in church or business. The Lord will pass over someone who spends time in front of an entertainment screen to look for someone who shows initiative and is not lazy. At first glance, it would appear that Elisha had no interest in prophetic ministry. Yet God sees the heart.

When it came time for a new king in Israel, all of Jesse's sons passed before the prophet Samuel yet none of them were qualified. God spoke to Samuel and said:

> *Don't judge by his appearance or height, for I have rejected him. The Lord doesn't see things the way you see them. People judge by outward appearance, but the Lord looks at the heart* (1 Samuel 16:7).

Remember the calling of John the Baptist? Zechariah and Elizabeth were unable to have children. Zechariah served in the rotation of priests at the temple of the Lord and an angel appeared to him, standing on the right side of the incense altar, which represents our prayer and intercession to Jesus. The Bible says Zechariah was shaken and overwhelmed with fear when he saw him. Why? Zechariah knew that oftentimes it was a sign of judgment when angels appeared. Zechariah said, "I'm dead. It's over."

The angel said to him, "Don't be afraid, Zechariah. God has heard your prayer." What prayer? Not the prayer he was praying in the temple that day. He was now an older man and was not praying about having kids. That time was already past. He had prayed that prayer when he and his wife were young. But what prayer was it? The answer came: "The prayer you prayed about having kids." Just because your prayer isn't answered today doesn't mean it's not going to be answered. Just because you think God didn't hear your prayer today doesn't mean God has forgotten.

> *Your wife, Elizabeth, will give you a son, and you are to name him John. You will have great joy and gladness, and many will rejoice at his birth, for he will be great in the eyes of the Lord. He must never touch wine or other alcoholic drinks. He will be filled with the Holy Spirit, even before his birth* (Luke 1:13-15).

Think about this for a moment. Even inside of the womb it's possible for a child to be filled with the power of the Holy Spirit because of how the parents are living!

> *And he will turn many Israelites to the Lord their God. He will be a man with the spirit and power of Elijah. He will prepare the people for the coming of the Lord. He will turn the hearts of the fathers to their children, and he will cause those who are rebellious to accept the wisdom of the godly* (Luke 1:16-17).

Zechariah didn't believe this word, and for nine months God removed his ability to talk. He did not want Zechariah speaking negatively about the promise of God that was going to take place!

Imagine you are the parents of John the Baptist, responsible to raise him in a godly atmosphere. John dressed and ate differently from everyone else and never seemed to fit in. Can't you hear someone in the neighborhood where they lived or from the synagogue they attended speaking about their concern for John's emotional well-being? He never went to the parties and didn't listen to the same music or watch the same movies. At school he read the Torah and the prophets. He was somewhat of a loner and not in

The Elijahs of God

the popular crowd. He never received the "most likely to succeed" award; he just graduated and disappeared from the watch list of society. But when John turned thirty years of age and opened his mouth, the whole nation wanted to hear what he had to say! Why? Because the spirit of Elijah came pouring out of his mouth to shake the nation.

> The Elijahs of God aren't interested in preserving their own legacy but understand that the mantle they possess must be transferred to continue the purpose of God.

I believe there is a call of God going forth right now to a generation that is being prepared to be anointed with power from on high! When Elisha began his ministry, all the sons of the prophets recognized what had happened to this young man.

> *When the group of prophets from Jericho saw from a distance what happened, they exclaimed, "Elijah's spirit rests upon Elisha!" And they went to meet him and bowed to the ground before him* (2 Kings 2:15).

Oh, hallelujah! Some of you reading this right now are sensing the power of God coming on you to speak in prophetic, last-days power! Don't be afraid of what the Lord desires to do in your life. You will confront the spirit of Jezebel in our land and be victorious!

The Elijahs of God aren't interested in preserving their own legacy but understand that the mantle they possess must be transferred to continue the purpose of God. As long as we act as though it's all about us, we'll be too insecure to empower the Elishas in our lives. They will never be willing to risk burning the plows of destiny if they can't trust us to let go of our own egos to see them succeed. We must also be willing to take a chance and grasp that the anointing and calling is generational. The prophet Malachi reminds us that the evidence of real revival is the spirit of Elijah that turns the hearts of fathers and children to each other:

I am sending you the prophet Elijah before the great and dreadful day of the Lord arrives. His preaching will turn the hearts of fathers to their children, and the hearts of children to their fathers. Otherwise I will come and strike the land with a curse (Malachi 4:5-6).

> **They will never be willing to risk burning the plows of destiny if they can't trust us to let go of our own egos to see them succeed.**

There are dreams in my heart that God intends to fulfill in my children and their seed for decades to come that can reverse any curse on the land. To the Elijahs of God reading this book, go find your Elishas and impart the heart of God to the next generation. To the Elishas of God, submit yourselves to the counsel and wisdom of your Elijah and learn to walk together until the voice of God thunders to the nations in Jesus' name!

As I close this book, I believe this is a prophetic word over your life:

You shall go forth in the spirit and power of Elijah and do exploits in My name. You shall see things prior generations could only dream about. Your voice shall speak in authority and grace as deliverance to the captives shall be your portion. You shall tear down the strongholds of darkness, release the captives, and declare freedom in Jesus' name. You shall raise up sons and daughters in the earth who will understand the sacrifices necessary to be in My counsel. You shall not wince at the enemy but be full of the might of the God of glory and march forward in step with the armies of heaven. The spirit of holiness, purity, repentance, and prayer shall characterize your life, and you will live in the peace of

The Elijahs of God

God, free from the shame of your past and besetting sins.
The life of an overcomer will cause you to move forward
in faith and your influence shall be great in the earth as
My hand rests upon you and guides your every step.

Now go forth, Elijahs of God!

Visit markivey.org to purchase.

This Special House

by Tiffany Ivey

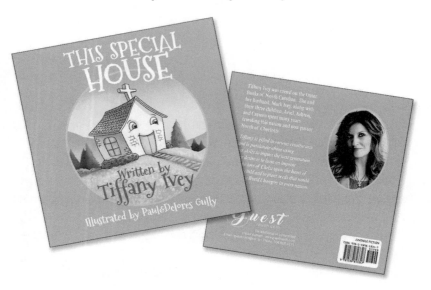

This Special House is an exciting new tool for churches to give to first-time guests and to make an investment in the next generation.

Churches can customize this kid's story on the cover, back, and body of the text with their own church's name, making it a great venue for both evangelism and ministry promotion. This Special House gives a clear presentation of Jesus in a fun, colorful book that kids and parents alike will treasure.

Visit www.guestreach.com for more information.

About the Author

Mark Ivey is a bold communicator of truth to this present generation. As an evangelist and now pastor of a growing church, he calls for Christians to passionately pursue spiritual awakening in the nations of the world and contend for biblical revival and supernatural invasion of God into every part of our culture. Mark and his wife Tiffany pastor Christ Alive Church in Newton, North Carolina. They have three children and have ministered to multiple thousands of people over the last thirty years.

Mark can be reached on Twitter: @markaivey or by visiting elijahsofgodmovement.com.

We are a Christian-based publishing company that was founded in 2009. Our primary focus has been to establish authors.

"5 Fold Media was the launching partner that I needed to bring *The Transformed Life* into reality. This team worked diligently and with integrity to help me bring my words and vision into manifestation through a book that I am proud of and continues to help people and churches around the world. None of this would have been possible without the partnership and education I received from 5 Fold Media."

- Pastor John Carter, Lead Pastor of Abundant Life Christian Center, Syracuse, NY, Author and Fox News Contributor

*The Transformed Life is foreworded by Pastor A.R. Bernard, received endorsements from best-selling authors Phil Cooke, Rick Renner, and Tony Cooke, and has been featured on television shows such as TBN and local networks

5 Fold Media
315.570.3333 | 5701 E. Circle Dr. #338, Cicero, NY 13039
manuscript@5foldmedia.com

Find us on Facebook, Twitter, and YouTube

Discover more at www.5FoldMedia.com.